Uncovering the World

Uncovering the World

Uncovering the World

*True Stories of Changed Lives
from Around the Globe*

Jonathan Carswell

Authentic

12 11 10 09 08 07 06 7 6 5 4 3 2 1

First published 2006 by Authentic Media
9 Holdom Avenue, Bletchley, Milton Keynes, Bucks, MK1 1QR, UK
285 Lynnwood Avenue, Tyrone, GA 30290, USA
OM Authentic Media, Medchal Road, Jeedimetla Village,
Secunderabad 500 055, A. P.
www.authenticmedia.co.uk
Authentic Media is a division of Send the Light Ltd., a company limited
by guarantee (registered charity no. 270162)

British Library Cataloguing in Publication Data

A catalogue record for this book is available
from the British Library

ISBN-13 978-1-85078-667-2
ISBN-10 1-85078-667-4

Please note that some of the names and personal details in this book
have been changed

Cover design by David McNeill
Print Management by Adare Carwin
Printed in Great Britain by J.H. Haynes & Co., Sparkford

Dedication

For my best friends: Mum and Dad

Thank you for keeping your promise to love, support and pray for me. You have never let me down.

Contents

Dedication   v
Acknowledgements   ix
Introduction   xi
Notes about Bible References   xiii

Jonathan, France   1
'I couldn't escape the torment of not having an answer'

Yu-re, South Korea   13
'You're demon possessed!'

Wenhao, China   24
'I was driven by ambition and achievement'

Nicola, Saudi Arabia   31
'The water engulfed me above and below'

Ville, Scandinavia   42
'It was the most humiliating experience of my life'

Tom, Ireland/France   52
'My degree was my god'

Ivy, China   64
'I thought I was OK as I was'

Matt, India   72
'I couldn't maintain the double life I was leading'

Jeiran, Azerbaijan   82
'I was lost. A battle was raging inside me'

Leanne, Finland   87
*'My mind was numb. I was always either drunk
or hung-over'*

A World of Difference   96
Further Reading   104
About Friends International   105
Key Passages in the Bible   108

Acknowledgements

Believe it or not, words have always troubled me. Getting the right words in the right place and meaning what I want them to, has been a taxing exercise for me ever since I learnt to write. I so often feel like the great orator (!) Winnie the Pooh who said, 'I am a bear of very little brain and long words trouble me!' I have thought long and hard about the words that I am about to write however, as I want to get them right, for I owe so much to each person mentioned.

To my family, who have always encouraged me with my writing; to Adrian and the family at HRBC, who gave me the time and space to write; Richard and Lizi at Friends International, who have been very patient with me as I failed to meet my deadlines; William Porter, for generously allowing me to squat in his cottage by the sea so that I might avoid the dreaded writer's block. To Charlotte at Authentic Media, for her belief in this project from the start; Mark Finnie, whose commitment to getting Christian books 'out there' is greatly appreciated; to each person in this book who has allowed me to write up their story, even though by doing so it put some of them in danger of persecution or abuse. I also want to thank my editor, Lucy. She has quickly, yet thoroughly, taken my many errors and shortcomings, and turned them into something of use.

Finally, thank *you,* the reader – may you see, as we 'uncover the world' how Jesus can transform your life.

Introduction

It was a daunting experience. For the first time in my life, I was travelling abroad without my parents. Unfortunately, I had not chosen to sail across the Channel and spend a relaxing week in the south of France; instead I had opted for a month of aid work in Thailand, a country and language I knew little about.

As I slowly made my way through customs, which involved my bags being searched (I think I must look very suspicious!), I stopped and wondered what I was doing. I panicked! What if something goes wrong? What if I become ill? What if I get taken away by bandits, or worse still what if no-one understands me when I order food and I starve to death? The thought of having no food for a month brought me out in a cold sweat! Before I knew it though, I was in a taxi and on my way to the village where I was staying. To my relief everything turned out fine. I didn't get ill, I wasn't taken away by bandits, and when all else failed McDonalds was always prepared to serve me a meal!

I guess that from my somewhat limited travels I might have experienced something of what you, an international student studying in the UK, might have experienced as you travelled here.

Time away is a great opportunity to explore and discover new things. I wonder if your studies here have ever caused you to think more about who you are, why you're here, if there is a God, and whether it really matters anyway?

Each story in this book is the true account of how international students during their time in the UK did just that – examined the claims of Jesus Christ for themselves.

All of the stories are different, but nevertheless true; and all those mentioned have come to the same life-changing conclusion.

For some it was a totally new idea, taking months of investigating the facts before they did anything about it; for others the story of Jesus was already familiar and they simply needed to respond to it. However, all of them came to realise that they needed Jesus, and allowed Him to make a difference in their lives.

You may be enjoying university life and taking pleasure in the experiences that a new culture brings, or you may be struggling to know the relevance of your life in a foreign country – whatever your situation, this book is designed to help you find the changing power of Jesus.

Notes about Bible References

If you have never read the Bible, or even looked through it, it can be quite confusing and daunting. It really doesn't need to be though.

There are 66 books that make up the Bible. The Bible is divided into two sections known as the Old Testament and the New Testament. The first four books of the New Testament, namely Matthew, Mark, Luke and John, are collectively known as the gospels.

Throughout *Uncovering the World* the Bible is mentioned in various different ways. Quite often it is quoted by the person who is telling their story. The quotation is marked with a footnote which gives reference to where it can be found in the Bible.

For example, a footnote saying Romans 3:23 means that the quotation is taken from the book of Romans. Each book in the Bible is divided into chapters and these are numbered. This is what the first number stands for. Then, each chapter is broken up into verses. These are also numbered. In the example above this is what the number 23 refers to. So if Romans 3:23 is referred to in one of the stories, this means that you can read the quotation in the Bible by turning to the book of Romans, chapter 3, and looking at verse 23.

Jonathan, France

'I couldn't escape the torment of not having an answer'

'Welcome to Newcastle International Airport. We hope you have enjoyed your flight with us, and hope to see you again. Have a very good evening.'

As the flight attendants welcomed passengers to the place that would be my home for the next 12 months, rain began to hit the cabin windows, smudging our view of the runway. The seatbelt sign had gone off and I was making my way down the plane steps with my rucksack and out towards customs.

'I doubt anyone from the university will come and meet me,' I thought to myself. 'After all, it is ten o'clock in the evening.'

When my bags eventually arrived on the carousel I found a trolley and headed towards the taxi rank. I was in a world of my own. I had been to England before, but never to live. I was slightly anxious about what the next few months would be like. Would I miss home? Would I crave *pain au chocolat*? Would I become increasingly lonely?

As these thoughts rushed through my mind I was brought back to reality when I saw two girls on the other side of the customs barrier. It wasn't the girls that necessarily caught my eye, but what they were holding: a white piece of paper with my name on it in black marker pen. 'Who are they and how do they know me?' I wondered. 'Why have they bothered to come and pick me up?' I had so many questions.

I went over and nervously introduced myself, slightly bewildered by who these two were. They were obviously students; you could tell by what they were wearing – that made me slightly more at ease. At least they weren't policemen wanting to deport me! They explained that they were from the Christian Union and they were helping international students settle into life at Newcastle University. I didn't really know what the Christian Union was, but I nodded politely and hopped in the car as they drove me to my hall of residence.

The girls made sure that I had everything I needed before leaving me in my room. They left me with their contact details if I needed any more help, said goodbye and shut the door behind them. For the first time since my arrival I was on my own. It was quite sobering. I was looking forward to the year ahead as a student though. Cheap beer, gigs and kebabs – this was the life! I wasn't aware of it, but my encounter with these two girls was the start of something that was to change my life…

I had arrived from a small town called Pau located at the base of the Pyrenees. The famous mountains were just 30 minutes drive from my door and I would regularly take a trip out to the foot of the mountains with my friends. Pau is most famous not for its location near the mountains, but for its Middle Age castle, where Henry IV was born. Even though I have been round the castle many times it still hasn't lost its grip on me. Its structure, shape and stature never bore me. And for those who like a party, Pau does not disappoint. The town is packed with international students and Thursday nights in the bars of the town are always interesting! I had come to England as part of my degree, and was hoping for a few good nights out in Newcastle too.

* * *

It was nearly six weeks after I had arrived. The weather was wetter and colder than when I had come on that dark night back in September. Jamie was, I thought, a typical English guy – he just looked English for a start! He was friendly, drank lots of tea and played football. Yet there was something different about him that really impressed me. He was a Christian. **He probably didn't know it, but his life and manner spoke volumes to me at the time.** He ran a coffee bar for international students every Monday night in a local church. I went along a few times and really enjoyed it, especially the chocolate fondue nights! While there I became good friends with a language student called Mark. He was a super guy; one of the nicest I have ever met. He was a Christian too. I couldn't understand it – every Christian I met seemed to be so nice, friendly and caring. Both Jamie and Mark seemed really keen to make sure I had a good time and went out of their way to help me. It seemed surreal, but I enjoyed it, and I got to know these two guys really well.

One Friday night I went out with Mark to an event run by the Christian Union. I had been to a couple of things at the church, but this was the first event which really made me think. At the end of the evening someone gave a talk about understanding who Jesus is, and how important it is to know Him. I must say, it made me feel slightly uncomfortable. Not that I didn't agree with what the speaker was saying; I knew he was right, and that troubled me, but I didn't understand who Jesus was. For years I had wondered what would happen when I died, and I knew this person Jesus had something to do with it. But **I had my whole life ahead of me – why think about it now?** And so I would push it to the back of my mind, something that I could worry about later. But recently I had been thinking about it much more, especially since meeting Jamie and Mark.

After the speaker had finished, we split up into small groups to pray. Pray?! I had no idea what I was meant to do. Being Roman Catholic I had prayed the Lord's Prayer and prayed to the virgin Mary before but that was about it. And those prayers were written down for me, whereas Mark and others in the group seemed to be praying whatever they liked. This was a totally new concept to me. There were four in our group; two of them had already prayed and the third was just starting. That meant that it was me next. I could feel the colour of my face dropping as I became pale and nervous. What was I supposed to pray? Was there something special and sacred that I was meant to say or could I pray something I knew, like the Lord's Prayer? Was I praying to Jesus, like the others had, or could I pray to Mary?

I have no idea what I prayed that night; looking back at it now I feel embarrassed! Thankfully, Mark who I knew quite well by then was reassuring, and the fact that he had prayed before me put me at ease.

After we had all prayed the meeting ended and one or two from our group drifted away. I stayed and collected a mug of coffee for Mark and myself. Free coffee and chocolate covered doughnuts – how could people walk away from that? Mark and I sat chatting for a while when he asked me a question that terrified me.

'Jonathan, if you died tonight, where would you go?'

I was shocked. Not just by the question, but the reality that it could happen tonight. My Religious Education lessons at school and my experience of the Roman Catholic Church had never probed me with such deep questions. Now however, these questions were constantly hounding me like a dog with a stick. **I couldn't escape the torment of not having an answer.** I had no idea where I would go. I hoped it would be heaven, but I wasn't sure. In fact I was far from sure. I was sure God existed – or at least I thought I was. Up until now I hadn't needed God anyway. I was a good guy, and it was only the bad ones that need saving by God, wasn't it? Wasn't that right? I no longer knew.

I tried to read bits of the New Testament but struggled; it just didn't compare to the pleasure of a good kebab from the local take-away after a night out in town. For me that was far more appealing. It didn't involve too much thinking and tasted good! However, I knew deep down that I had to find an answer.

Before long it was the end of term and I was due to return to my home town, Pau for Christmas. How could I walk away from life in Newcastle now though? I had had such a wonderful time: experiencing British culture, exploring Christianity, and partying in some of the busiest nightclubs in the North. No, I couldn't walk away now. Whilst I was looking forward to seeing friends and family, I knew that I couldn't dismiss the issue of Christianity… yet. I would be back, and I knew that it wouldn't be long until I was.

* * *

I arrived back in early February; the cold bite of winter taking its full effect on my body. Goose bumps were appearing all over my arms as I queued with my friends to enter a nightclub in Newcastle. Nothing much had changed. Yes, Christmas had come and gone and the New Year celebrations were over, but the beer was still cheap, the kebabs just as greasy and tasty, and not to my surprise, the Christians were still as friendly as they had ever been. My two friends, Jamie and Mark, were still around and forever pressing me to come along to another Christian event with them. I would happily oblige. While I never thought that becoming a Christian was something for me I did really enjoy hanging out with them. Their religion intrigued me – it seemed to have a huge impact on their everyday life.

Valentine's Day had just passed when I went along to an event held in one of the halls of residence. It was what they called a 'Grill a Christian'. I thought it might involve a barbecue – but I was wrong! When the meeting began, a panel of Christians took their seats at the front, facing the awaiting audience, and prepared to be bombarded with questions from the crowd. I didn't ask any questions myself, and to be honest, I can't really remember much of the discussion that went on. After the question time had finished through, I got talking to a guy from Wales called Will. He was a big guy, and at 6 foot 2, he towered over me. I hadn't met anyone from Wales before, and I had to listen really carefully to understand him. He spoke quickly with a strong accent. Even my English friends struggled to understand him sometimes!

We hadn't been chatting long when he invited me along to a Bible study happening later on that week, run especially for international students. I had to rearrange my plans but accepted; I thought it might be a nice thing to do.

* * *

We were sat around the table talking when we read together a sentence from the Bible: 'This is a true saying, and everyone should believe it: Christ Jesus came into the world to save sinners.'[1] I read the sentence again to make sure I had understood it correctly. **Jesus, the man who claimed to be God, came to die...*for me?* My head spun as I tried to understand what that meant.** For the last hour, Will and another guy had been trying to show us the evidence from the Bible that proved Jesus was God. I had just about grasped what they were saying, but if this was true, then this fact – that He came to die for me, was mind blowing. 'Why did He do it?' I thought to myself. 'He was God, He could have refused and punished us all. **Why go to all that trouble?**'

I raised my questions to the group and Will encouraged us to look at a section of the Bible. 'This part is an accurate biography of Jesus' life,' he told us, 'and there is a sentence in here that will help us with Jonathan's questions, I think. It shows what Jesus was going through before He died, but most importantly it shows His obedience to His Father.'

Once everyone had found the page we were reading, Will read the sentence aloud: '"Father," he said, "everything is possible for you. Please take this cup of suffering away from me. Yet I want your will, not mine."'[2]

Will read it to us again and then looked up. 'Does that help?' he said as he looked at me, while also spinning his pen round in his hand. 'Jesus died because it was all part of God's plan for mankind. God wanted to give us a second chance and so He allowed His Son to die for us.'

'I think it does. Thanks,' I said. 'This is how I understand it. Jesus died for me voluntarily because if He

---

[1] 1 Timothy 1:15 (NLT)
[2] Mark 14:36 (NLT)

hadn't, I would have to find a way to pay for the punishment I deserve for doing wrong things. Am I right?'

'Yes! That's it!' Will said, excited and slightly surprised that I had finally understood what he was talking about.

The discussion continued that night as Will and his friend explained why Jesus had to die. It was all new to me. Even at school or Mass it had never been explained to me like this. It was making much more sense now but I needed to know more. I was certain that Jesus was someone special; I now knew that He died on my behalf so that I could escape punishment. But I wasn't ready to become a Christian yet.

Looking at the lifestyle that Will and Mark and others had, I knew that to become a Christian didn't involve the signing of a legal document, joining a club or merely saying you were a Christian. It affected everything, and they said it would need to do the same to me. This wasn't something I could do on Sundays or just when I felt I needed God, but I needed to be committed to God, just as He is committed to me.

As I made my way home that night, kicking a stone along the pavement as I went, I was amazed that God should die for me. Why would He do that? What had I got to offer? I had spent my teenage and student years drinking cheap beer, eating dodgy kebabs and flirting with girls – why would He be bothered with me?

Over the coming weeks more and more of Jesus' life was explained to me as we studied Mark's Gospel. I tried again to read my Bible, and although I found it hard, it did help me to understand the purpose of Jesus' life on earth. In the section of the Bible we read together, Mark, the writer, records one of the statements that Jesus makes about becoming a Christian.

Jesus said, *'If anyone would come after me, he must deny himself and take up his cross and follow me. For whoever wants to save his life will lose it, but whoever loses his life for me and for the gospel will save it.'*[3] The more that I read, the more I knew that becoming a Christian would have serious implications for my life. In the international study group we talked about the lifestyle of a Christian and how it was to be different from that of somebody who did not follow Jesus. In the coming days and weeks, as the evidence for Jesus and His message mounted up, I knew I was going to have to make a big decision. Was I prepared to give up the life that I enjoyed so much for the sake of following Jesus Christ? Questions still buzzed around in my head, but would they ever be answered? And did they need to be answered before I could fully put my trust in Jesus? I just didn't know.

It was time to talk to Will again! Although I had a thousand and one other questions, the one I wanted the answer for most was: do I need all the answers before becoming a Christian? If Will's answer was yes then I had a lot of work to do – and wasn't sure I would ever have them all.

Thankfully, as Will and I chatted over email, he explained that I would never have all the answers to my questions. If I did, God would not be God, and I would not be human. He pointed out to me a verse in the Bible which says: 'As you do not know the path of the wind, or how the body is formed in a mother's womb, so you cannot understand the work of God, the Maker of all things.'[4]

I needed to make a decision. I couldn't sit on the fence anymore, nor could I protest my innocence or plead my ignorance. Would I admit I'd done wrong, that I'd rejected Jesus in the way that I'd lived and

---

[3] Mark 8:34
[4] Ecclesiastes 11:5

done what I pleased, or would I continue to live for myself?

For some reason I failed to make the decision that night. Whatever it was, something distracted me, and God, His forgiveness and its impact on my life was soon out of mind. It was party time again.

* * *

She was gorgeous! She had a sexy French accent and a body to match. I was leaving for home in a few weeks but what did it matter? Who would it hurt? For me there was always time for a quick fling with a good-looking girl.

We had a great time together. A great kisser and good fun, this was my kind of girl! But of course it didn't last. It was never going to, and I knew that. As I made my way home following another empty evening, I was filled with loneliness, self-pity and regret as tears of sorrow began to roll down my face. My eyes were red and my cheeks were wet. I couldn't remember the last time I cried. As I lay flat on my bed, trying to regain my dignity, I knew that it was not another romance that I needed but the forgiveness, love, and life-changing peace that was offered in a relationship with Jesus Christ.

'God, you know the dreadful state that I am in. I have refused to answer your call to me. I know I have to respond to it, and I want to do that now. Please will you forgive me, change me and make me a new person, who lives for you rather than for my own pleasures? I can't do this on my own. I need your help. I have done so many wrong things and I deserve to be punished for them but I thank you that Jesus has paid the price for them when He died on the cross. I am so excited that by praying this prayer and you forgiving me, I have been saved from your judgment and have been brought into a living relationship with you. I cannot thank you enough. Thank you for hearing this prayer.'

I lay on my bed as still as I could. The tears appeared again as I considered the cost of Jesus dying on the cross, and the fact that He did it for me. Nothing dramatically changed that night, but as I leaned over to turn out my bedside light I couldn't help but smile, knowing that I had peace with the God who made me, loves me, and died for me so that one day I would spend all eternity with Him.

* * *

It wasn't long before I was heading back to France to continue my studies. In France I didn't know anyone who was a Christian, and so there weren't people with whom to study the Bible. I spent a lot of time with Will and the others before leaving, and did my best to learn as much of the Bible as I could. I knew it was going to be hard returning to France. But my life had changed since that eventful night a few months ago. Most of the tears had dried up, but I was a new person! My life had changed; my lifestyle was dramatically different. OK, I still enjoyed cheap, greasy kebabs, but rather than living for my own self-indulgence I was now living for God. I was trying to live out what a verse in the Bible says: 'The Lord knows who his people are. So everyone who worships the Lord must turn away from evil.'[5] Because I was serious about living for Jesus my life had to dramatically change. Unfortunately, and to my surprise, it didn't happen overnight. There were times when I made dreadful mistakes, let my language slip, or just chose to do my own thing. Each time I was left feeling disgusted and

---

[5] 2 Timothy 2:19 (CEV)

disappointed with myself. I had let God down, and I had spoilt my relationship with Him.

The Christian life is a series of fresh starts however, and **God loves us all so much that He continues to take us back.** I have supreme confidence in the fact that although I continue to do wrong, the goodness, love, and forgiveness of Jesus is much, much greater. So much so that my sinfulness does not rule my life but rather the goodness of God is evident in my life because of the difference He has made within me.[6]

* * *

Jonathan is now a theological student in his home country of France, just outside Paris (he can't get enough of student discounts!). In the coming years he hopes to work with French Christian Unions, helping them tell students about the life-changing message of Jesus.

---

[6] See Romans 5:14–15

Yu-re, South Korea

'You're demon possessed!'

'You're demon possessed!' He grabbed me and said it again a little louder. He had a tennis racket in his left hand and a tight grip of me in his right. We were outside the house, near the end of the garden path by the gate. He swung the tennis racket down hitting me. I let out a loud shriek – a mixture of pain and shock. Again, he brought the racket down, striking me across my legs. I bruised immediately.

'OK, OK!' I moaned, 'I won't go again.'

My father immediately loosened his grip and released me. He had been granted his wish – I wouldn't be going to church again.

* * *

In many ways, I was an ordinary girl from Seoul, South Korea. My parents valued family life greatly, and rewarded effort and achievement while punishing failure and weakness. I was the oldest, and so the pressure was on me to do well. Academic achievement was the most important thing, according to my parents. They hoped that their eldest daughter would lift the family name of

Bae up high. Unfortunately, despite being diligent in all I did, I was not 'clever enough' to satisfy them. I grew up to be a very unhappy and dissatisfied girl. **I longed for somebody to depend upon; somebody whom I could love; somebody who would love me back.**

Even at the age of twelve I remember tossing and turning in my bed, struggling to sleep. It was more than just the restlessness of a young adolescent. I was suffering from stress. My nights were interrupted by nightmares. I would wake up in the cold sweats of panic.

One day somebody suggested an unusual insomnia remedy. They said I should repeat 'Jesus' over and over before going to sleep. I had no idea why they suggested this, but I thought I would try it. I did, and to my surprise it worked. As a result I began to read the Bible. My parents weren't keen on me doing this but, I learned to hide my Bible when they came into my room to say goodnight. At this stage though it was merely a remedy to sleep better and calm my nerves under the pressure of school study. When I was doing well I ignored God, but when the pressure was on (around exam time!) I blamed God. In the six years of school that followed I read the Old Testament twice and the New Testament several times; but still Jesus meant nothing to me.

As I completed my final year at school I began the usual process of applying to university. I was called for an interview at a couple of universities in Seoul. After one interview I remember how I got lost in the huge campus. I had absolutely no idea how to get out or where the tube station was. Plucking up some courage, I asked a girl for directions. She kindly offered to take me to the station. It was a ten-minute walk, and as we chatted she asked me whether I went to church. I explained that I had just started to go to a church close to my home. I told her that my parents were not keen for me to go; however, because I had finished my final exam they said I could go.

Her next question confused and slightly unnerved me.

'Are you sure that when this life ends you are a forgiven person, forgiven by God?'

Her question was a shock. Why did I have to be forgiven? I knew there was a gulf between me and God; however, I understood that the way of bridging the gap was by being good. I hoped that by constantly pleasing God I would get closer to Him. I wasn't sure whether it was working or not; I guessed that it wasn't.

That same afternoon, she asked if I wanted to know what the Christian message was all about. Why not? I thought. I had a free afternoon and so I accepted her invitation. We chatted as we changed direction from the train station to an empty seminar room. Ji-Hea opened a Bible and showed me a short paragraph which explained that I could do nothing to get closer to God. Good behaviour was not enough – God wasn't interested in me trying to be good. I could never be good enough for His perfect standard; He required something different.

For the next hour Ji-Hea explained to me who Jesus was, and why He came to this earth.

'It is our wrongdoing, our sin, which cuts us off from God, and the reason it cuts us off is because He is perfect and pure. If we were to take our sin into heaven it would dirty and spoil something that is clean and perfect. He cannot tolerate any wrongdoing. However much we try to cover or correct our sin we simply cannot do it. The Bible teaches that sin must be punished. It has to be removed and we are unable do this. The first man and woman, Adam and Eve, were told that if they disobeyed God they would "surely die."[7] This is exactly what

---

[7] Genesis 2:17

happened. They disobeyed God and in every way possible they died. Their perfect and harmonious relationship with God came to an end; it died. Physically, they also died – not immediately, but over time until eventually their life ended.'

Ji-Hea reassured me that this was not the end of the Christian message. 'If it was,' she said with a smile, 'there would be nothing good about Christianity. It would be all very depressing.' Thankfully, there was more to come.

* * *

Each week Ji-Hea and I would meet for one hour to look at the Bible together. Even after I left university we continued meeting. I was intrigued and interested, and wanted to know more. I was amazed at the wisdom in the Bible; sometimes it was common sense, other times I had to question whether men could pen these spiritual truths. I needed to know more. I had many questions and I needed the answers.

One week, Ji-Hea flicked over the pages of her Bible to a book called Hebrews. She read this sentence to me: 'Without blood, to represent death, there can be no forgiveness of sin.'[8] She went on, **'This is why Jesus came – He came to die. He came to give His blood so that we could be forgiven.** Only Jesus could do this, for only Jesus is perfect. Jesus' blood is more than enough to cover all of our wrong.'

We were both smiling. For the first time in my life I realised that I could be free from the punishment I deserved; free also from the guilt that came with it. Jesus' sacrificial death meant that God could forgive the wrongdoing which ruled my life. He could take charge of

---

[8] Hebrews 9:22 (paraphrased)

my life and change me and make me perfect in His sight. But that's not all; one day, when I died, He was going to allow me to be with Him in heaven, forever![9]

'Why don't you come to some evening events that are being run in the city this week?' Ji-Hea asked. 'They'll help you understand more about the good news of Jesus and I think you'll really enjoy them. I'm going. You're welcome to join me.'

I went along for three consecutive nights. The significance of Jesus' death for us was explained again, every night. The speaker told us simply how Jesus not only died but three days later, just as He had promised, He came back to life.[10] Amazing! Jesus came back to life! Once again, it proved that He was no ordinary man. Over the course of these talks the speaker explained the importance of the resurrection.

'The resurrection of Jesus is crucial to the Christian belief,' the speaker explained to us. 'It gives every believer a certainty for the future. By rising from the dead Jesus guaranteed a place in heaven for every one of His followers. His death means that we have the opportunity to accept His forgiveness. If we do, we are seen as perfect in God's sight. Because of this, we are welcomed into heaven – a place where only those without sin in God's eyes can go.'

It was exciting to hear heaven talked about like this. I was being told there was a place guaranteed for everyone who believes in Him. I wanted a place saved for me.

The speaker continued. 'Such hope and assurance allows all Christians to have confidence in death, because we know that it is not the end. As Paul, a writer of many of the letters in the New Testament said, "Death [is]

---

[9] See Romans 6:21–23
[10] See Mark 9:31

swallowed by triumphant Life! Who got the last word, oh, Death? Oh, Death, who's afraid of you now?"[11] The resurrection of Jesus is the triumphant and glorious victory for every believer in Jesus, the man who died, was buried, and came back to life again – as the Bible said He would. And, He will return to earth! Those who die believing in Jesus will be brought back to life to live with Jesus forever; not reincarnated, but brought back to life – with perfect new bodies.'

I had been convicted throughout the three meetings. However, it was on the third and final evening that I was really challenged to do something about it. The death of Jesus was a personal gift for me, Yu-re Bae. With tears streaming down my cheeks I prayed:

'Dear Father, I am sorry that I have sinned, rebelled against You and offended You deeply, but I'm really glad You have loved me. Thank You so much for sending your Son Jesus, to die in my place, taking my punishment. Now I can be free from my sin and be friends with You. There is nothing that I could do to make this happen, but thankfully You have done it all through your Son Jesus. **Please will you take charge of my life tonight**? Thank you. Amen.'

On that cloudy night, in late April, nearly a year after having met Ji-Hea, I became a Christian. I knew the impact that this would bring, especially on my family life, but I was prepared to put aside those fears for the sake of being forgiven by the Almighty, loving, Heavenly Father who was God.

* * *

---

[11] 1 Corinthians 15:54b–55 (The Message)

My life was changed forever that night. I was so excited to go to church and hear the talks from the Bible, meet new friends and learn more about Jesus. Getting to know God better and talking to Him through prayer was amazing. I had great contentment knowing that I was a forgiven person – something I had never had before.

My sister came along to church with me a couple of times, but I don't think she really enjoyed it. My parents were extremely worried that I had become involved with a cult. These are common in South Korea and in some ways I can understand why they were concerned. There was nothing cultish about my relationship with Jesus though. However, it was difficult to explain this to them without them going to church for themselves. A further concern that my parents had was the hour's travel I had to do each way by tube to get to church with Ji-Hea. Despite these concerns they did let me go, and most weeks I would stay for lunch after church.

One week, as I was eating lunch, my mobile phone rang. It was my Dad demanding that I come back home; they had decided they did not want me to go to church any more. I didn't rush home but went back later that evening after playing football with some friends from church. When I arrived home my Mum and Dad ordered me to sit in the living room. They urged me not to go back. 'It's a cult,' they kept saying. I tried to explain that the church I was involved in was a conventional mainstream church.

They were not prepared to listen; I was told never to go again. My Dad's eyes began to well up with tears as he gave the orders; such was his desire for me not to go back. The consequences were clear: if I chose to disobey my parents they would disown me. It was at this point that my Dad attacked me with the tennis racket. I desperately wanted to go back to church, but my only escape from my

Dad's attack was to say I wouldn't go again. And so I agreed. At that, my Dad dropped the tennis racket, thanked me and began to cry. I ran straight to my room, shut the door, and burst into tears. My body was aching, not so much from the bruises on my arms, legs and stomach, but because I had failed to stand up to what I believed in the face of this abuse.

The following Sunday I picked up my handbag, placed my Bible inside it, and made my way to church. When I arrived home my family demanded to know where I had been. My parents had put my sister in charge of always knowing where I went. She was desperate to find me, angry with me that I'd been to church again. She started to insult me, hitting me with her fists. I tried to remember a sentence from the Bible which says: 'If you're abused because of Christ, count yourself fortunate. It's the Spirit of God and His glory in you that brought you to the notice of others… if it's because you're a Christian, don't give it a second thought. Be proud of the distinguished status reflected in that name!'[12]

My parents once again urged me not to go back to the church. They threatened to go and scold the minister and disfigure my friend. They also warned me that they would take away all my possessions and withdraw me from university. They then said something which would haunt me for days: 'Yu-re, if you go back to church my mother and I will commit suicide.'

It was so tempting to give up being a Christian, stop going to church, and deny my faith in God. However, I knew I couldn't, because doing so would be rejecting the forgiveness of God and the eternal life He offers. I found it so hard to continue under the hostility of my family. I knew though, that

---

[12] 1 Peter 4:14, 16 (The Message)

however difficult the abuse was, God would always be with me. He promised never to leave us. Again, another sentence from the Bible came to my mind: 'Dear Friends, do not be surprised at the painful trial you are suffering, as though something strange were happening to you. But rejoice that you participate in the suffering of Jesus, so that you may be overjoyed when His glory is revealed.'[13]
What I faced at that time seemed out of control, so difficult to understand, yet I knew I was not suffering by myself. Those first four months after I became a Christian were the hardest of my life, but I'm thankful to God that He strengthened and matured me in my faith.

A few weeks later, I decided that I would stand up for what I believed and go to church. Once more, I explained to my parents why I wanted to go and why they need not worry about me. My Dad was very angry. He told me he had already lost his daughter, but this pushed him over the edge. He took a knife in the kitchen, and clasping me close to him, he held it to my neck telling me he would kill me if I went to church. I was petrified. What could I do? If I disobeyed him again he was going to slit my throat; yet every inch of my body wanted to stand up for what I believed. Once again, I met his demands and said I wouldn't go to church.

* * *

A month later an opportunity to learn more about the Bible came up. It was a church weekend, where many students like me would be going. I really wanted to go. I mentioned it to my mother who emphatically said I couldn't. I was entering another battle, torn between

---

[13] 1 Peter 4:12–13

doing what I believed to be right, and between obeying my parents. I had to make a decision now that I was eighteen: would I accept my parents' wishes even though they were contrary to what God would have me do? I was happy to obey my parents in everything, provided that what they wanted didn't contradict what God wanted. Standing up to my angry father was a scary thing to do, yet I knew that the most important thing was to obey God. God is greater than my Dad, and one day my father would have to give an account of his actions.

I *did* go on the weekend conference. I had an excellent time, learning more about God. I called my mother to tell her I was OK and that she needn't worry, for I had left without telling them. My mother cried over the phone and pleaded with me to come back. However, I had to hang up, as once again, she threatened to commit suicide if I did not return home. It was at this point that my parents realised that I would not give up on my faith, despite the various threats. They decided that the only thing to do was to send me to a foreign country.

Graciously, they asked where I wanted to go. The only other language I could speak, other than my home dialect, was English. This narrowed the options. It was either America, Australia, New Zealand, Canada, England or South Africa. The first three were ruled out as I would need to apply for a visa in advance. Therefore, as we were making the decision in late August, the UK seemed a good option. As I didn't need to apply for a visa, I would be able to get into the country without a problem.

So in early September of that same year I arrived on UK soil for the first time. It was an emotional time leaving my parents, unsure of the future and whether I would see them again. However, I knew that the stand I was making was right. I had come to learn English for a few months before applying to the University of Hull to do a Masters in politics. Thankfully, I was accepted, and before long I was on my way to graduating.

Coming to England hasn't been an easy experience at all. Leaving my home, friends and family was extremely difficult. Yet to me, to live for Jesus means everything; even if that means the loss of my family because they don't share the same belief. Jesus has made a world of difference in my life. He's forgiven my wrongdoing; **He's given me the hope of heaven when I die, and a purpose to live for today.**

Yu-re is still living in England, as her parents remain hostile towards her. She is now the international student worker at a church in Hull.

Wenhao, China

'I was driven by ambition and achievement'

From as early as I can remember I was driven by ambition and achievement – almost to a level of obsession. I grew up in China and was always diligent with my studies. I was committed to doing the best that I possibly could. However, being ambitious had its downside. I was never content with life and it frustrated me that despite being so devoted to the things I was involved in, I was always left somewhat empty.

I was a free thinker. I believed that there were super-beings, maybe gods; but I was not sure whether there was a life after death, which threw the whole idea of there being a God into disarray. Being brought up and educated to be a Communist confused me further. I joined the Communist party for myself at the age of twenty-six when I was doing my Masters in the coastal city of Dalian, northeast China. The requirements to join the party were: a) a belief in Communism; b) a recognition of the Chinese Communist party as leader of the Chinese people working for the best interests of the Chinese people; c) a love for the Chinese Communist party; and d) a willingness to sacrifice myself for the best interests of the party and the Chinese people. Whilst I agreed to each of these points I wasn't really involved. I was more of a nominal member, and definitely not the most committed!

Whilst studying for my English degree at Dalian, **I had searched for the meaning of life.** I tried looking at philosophy books rather than religious ones. I thought religions were for emotionally weak people. However, none of the philosophy books that I read could persuade me that this life was meaningful, or that I had a purpose to life. As a twenty-six year old that made me feel so lost: I couldn't understand why people were suffering in their lives; I couldn't cope with the many trivial things that I had to do every day. I was in a bit of a mess.

* * *

I arrived in the UK in early October of the same year to study for a PhD at the University of Southampton. It was a dramatic and significant change in my life for many reasons. Thankfully, it began the process of clearing up the dreadful mess and confusion in my mind and in my life.

As my search for meaning and purpose continued, so did my studies. I hadn't really thought that coming to England would give me an opportunity to explore religion further, let alone Christianity. One day **I noticed a sign** while wandering around the city. **It was outside a church advertising a course with the slogan: 'What is the meaning of life?' It was directed at me!** That was the exact question on my mind. Without hesitation I walked into the church and signed up for the course starting the following week.

The people on the course were from different backgrounds and of different ages. Those running the course shared with us personal stories of their lives. Their way of looking at life and people was enlightening – they were Christians. I had a wonderful time, meeting them and getting to know them. It was great to learn how the Bible explains the meaning of life. I was surprised at first to find so many answers in a book which I had never considered before. We were told how Jesus died for us, came back to life and can transform everyone's life. I must say, I was intrigued to know why it was necessary for a man to die in order for me to have life – it puzzled me. None of the philosophers I had read had ever mentioned anything like this, and yet I reminded myself that neither had they given me any hope. What I was learning on this course was giving me hope, but it still wasn't real to me. I wasn't yet convinced.

As part of the course we had a weekend away. I was intrigued to see how Christians lived differently. Their lifestyle was consistent with what they believed: the two went together. I was so convinced by seeing their way of life, and the passion for what they believed that I began to read the Bible for myself. Little by little, as I read short sections of the New Testament, I learned more about Jesus. His life was even more amazing than the Christians I had recently met. He never did anything wrong but went around changing lives! He was radical, but not in a strange way. I read how He ate and talked with tax collectors, forgave a woman caught in adultery, chose twelve ordinary men to be His disciples and taught people to love their enemies. Who was this man? I wanted to know more. It was during this weekend away that I finally understood how my life could have meaning and purpose. It wasn't about what *I* could do, but about what Jesus had done for me. I began to believe that Jesus had died for me so that I could be free. Through His dying, He brought me life through the forgiveness of my sins.

What Jesus achieved for me was totally different from any of the other religions or philosophies I had studied. Jesus was the only one who died for me. He died so that I might see me as good. God loved me so much that He was willing to send His Son to die in my place. As the Bible says, 'the trademark of all his work is love.'[14] Our 'fateful dilemma is resolved…[we] no longer have to live under a continuous, low-lying black cloud'[15] before God; but now, 'Christ, like a strong wind, has magnificently cleared the air, freeing [us] from a fated lifetime of brutal tyranny at the hands of sin and death.'[16] It was by His death that 'Christ died for sins once for all, the righteous for the unrighteous, to bring [us] to God.'[17]

This, we were told, was the meaning of life – to come back into a personal, enjoyable, and permanent relationship with God, the creator of this world. I was so excited! **For someone who had struggled to find the meaning to life, here it was!** Becoming a Christian wasn't for the emotionally weak but for those who realised their sinful condition before God. There and then I prayed to God, asking Him to be my Saviour; to come into my life, change me and refine me so that I might be less like me and more like Him. My face beamed, for in Jesus I had found meaning and purpose. Jesus had done it all for me. There was nothing that I could have done to work my way to God. He had to come and rescue me. My sin was a barrier between God and me. Nothing but Jesus' death could break it down. He came to save me – all that was left for me to do was accept His free gift of forgiveness and rescue.

---

[14] Psalm 145:17 (The Message)
[15] Romans 8:1,2a (The Message)
[16] Romans 8:2b (The Message)
[17] 1 Peter 3:18

At the end of the weekend all the participants were encouraged to attend church regularly. 'Coming to church will not transform your life,' we were told, 'but it will give you further opportunities to explore what the Christian life is all about.'

'Of course I'm going to go to church,' I thought to myself. Jesus had changed my life and I wanted to know more about Him. I continued to read my Bible as I had began doing on the weekend away. Just a section every day, but it was really helping me to understand more of what God was like. I was still as driven by my work as ever before, however now it wasn't for my own satisfaction, but for God's pleasure. I was still tempted by my old beliefs. I found it very difficult to understand how this world was created by God for example. While I still had many questions though, the more I read of the Bible the more questions were answered. God was proving Himself to me through the Bible.

* * *

The following summer I suffered from a difficult period of depression. This was going to really put my faith in God to test. Was He just a temporary interest in my life or was He really my Lord and Saviour?

I found comfort in talking to Christian friends and reading the Bible. It was a long time before I improved, but God remained faithful to me throughout my illness. Following my recovery, I realised more than ever that I needed Jesus in my life, and that He indeed is my Saviour. **Without committing my life to Him,** praying and talking to Him, **I would never have survived. He brought me true and full life.**

I had found it hard to tell my family and friends about my new-found faith, so I had tried to keep it quiet up to this point. I was afraid that they may be disappointed with me, and I was worried about what they would say. It was shortly after my depression that I told my parents and friends that I was a Christian. My parents found it difficult to understand what I meant. They thought I had been brainwashed and that I was under the control of a cult group. But when I returned to China that summer, having completed my studies, I was able to show them just what a difference Jesus had made in my life. I showed them my Chinese Bible, and talked about Jesus. I pointed out some of the sentences from the New Testament, and to my surprise my mother became interested. She had a Buddhist background and had always believed in the gods. But during those summer weeks my mother began to realise that Jesus was the only one who could offer life through the forgiveness of sins. She too became a Christian later that summer.

Looking back at my life since I became a Christian, I think God is really amazing. He has blessed me so much that **I cannot think of a single day when I haven't enjoyed His love.**

* * *

Wenhao is now working with her church in Southampton. She is involved in a one-year course aimed at helping Christians tell their friends and family about Jesus. She says, 'I enjoy the course so much. It has taught me how to articulate what Jesus has done for people in the world. It has given me great confidence in telling people who feel lost and are still searching for the meaning of life that Jesus loves them. The way that Jesus has transformed my life is so significant that I can't help but tell people about it. Jesus Himself told us that we should tell everyone about Him – and that's what I want to do.[18] *Just as I*

---

[18] Matthew 28:19–20

was encouraged to do, I want to help people to come to Jesus; He is the way, He is the truth, and He is the life!'

If you are interested in finding out about where you can join a course that will help you investigate who Jesus is then why not look at: www.christianityexplored.com or email: info@new2uk.org

Nicola, Saudi Arabia

'The water engulfed me above and below'

I remember the day in question. The sun was beaming down on the cool, calm water. My father, who had done well in the oil industry, had arranged for the family to join a company excursion on the Sun Moon Lake in central Taiwan. We were there for five days: days that were meant to help us relax, spend time together as a family, and provide memories we would never forget.

We were sitting towards the back on the top deck of the cruiser boat. The guide was drawing our attention to various places of interest with some facts and statistics. At five and eight years of age, my brother and I were more interested in seeing the animals that lined the banks of the lake, or seeing the fish leap out of the water in an attempt to catch any low-flying insects. Mum held onto us as we leaned over the edge trying to get a better view.

It was then that it happened. Out of nowhere, and for no reason the boat rocked sharply and violently as it would have done on a stormy day. The boat was out of control. After what seemed like minutes but in reality was a split second, the boat flipped over, tossing us into the deep water below.

The water engulfed me above and below. **I was starved of oxygen and I began to panic.** Mum and Dad were not there to help. I was on my own. I could see people and debris everywhere. I tried to swim up towards the surface, but as I did so I collided with something, crashing my head against it. Blood from my head hit the water, spreading suddenly and dyeing the water like food colouring. I tried to swim down to find an alternative way of escape. From that moment on I don't remember much else until a bright light shone in my direction. It was the search and rescue team. They rescued me and a dozen other casualties that hadn't been able to swim to safety.

Surprisingly, I wasn't as scared as I might have thought. Being so young and naive I thought everyone would be OK. Yet as I looked around, Robert and Mum were nowhere to be seen. 'Where were they?… Were they safe?… Had they been taken to hospital?… Were they still in the water?' Questions bombarded my throbbing head. **I was confused, shocked and scared. Deep down though, I still thought that everything would be OK.** Mum and Robbie would be found and helped to shore, and we would return to our hotel with an amazing story to tell our friends and relatives.

That night however it was just Dad and I who returned to the hotel. It was a lonely, sleepless night. I was restless with shock. I felt so weak I couldn't even cry – however much I wanted to. I clutched onto my duvet; longing for the comfort of my mother's arms.

I was woken up the next morning with the sound of my Dad on the telephone. I felt sick as I rubbed my eyes, stretching for the alarm clock beside my bed. It was only 7:27, yet surprisingly I was wide awake. The trauma of last night was still engulfing me. I walked towards the window that overlooked the lake. A light mist hovered over the still, calm water. There was what looked like a fisherman on the other side of the lake. Who else would sit on the bank of a lake at 7:30am? He seemed to be waving. Perhaps he was waving at me. Had he found a body? Two bodies? Had Mum and Robert been found…?

My hopes of them being found alive never became a reality. It was two days later, on the Monday, that little Robbie was found. It was the 27th of August, and it would have been his sixth birthday. Mum was found a day later. They were of course both dead.

* * *

The memories I have of that day are in some ways so vivid, yet in many ways so vague and incomplete. I remember the silly things that an eight-year-old would be worried about in that situation, like not wanting to lose my favourite jumper which was tied loosely around my waist. Over time the memories came back to me, although I sometimes wonder if they are a result of my mind working overtime. Either way, the tragic events of that day were real. They happened. And for the rest of my life I would have to live with the consequences of them.

It wasn't long before a number of family members flew out to see us. Times like these were not to be spent alone, but around the ones we loved. My Dad's brother quickly joined us with his wife, and in the coming months they became my guardians. I travelled back with them to Britain, while my Dad remained mostly in Taiwan. Moving around was nothing new – my parents had moved four times in Saudi Arabia before I was five. The next few months Dad was occupied with the legal proceedings and coordination of his move back to the UK. It was in November that he went back home and I returned into his care. We moved into a place of our own in Oxfordshire along with a lovely lady called Debbie who was to become my future stepmother.

Life in the UK was different from what I had experienced in any of the other countries I had lived in. When we were in Saudi Arabia we didn't really bother with church as a family – Mum and Dad had taught me good morals and values, but that is about where it stopped. However, now we were in the UK church was one of those things that we did together every Easter and Christmas. I had always believed in God, but never really knew what that meant. It didn't have any impact on my young, eventful life and so I guess, if I am honest, it meant nothing at all. Anyway, **if there was Someone up there why had He taken my Mum and Robbie from us?**

My attendance at church dramatically changed however, when I began to attend an all girls' Church of England boarding school, where attendance at chapel was mandatory six times a week, every week of the year. If that wasn't going to change a girl's opinion of God's existence, or His relevance, then I guess nothing would!

As I seem to remember, it wasn't long before I revised my initial feelings about God, coming to believe (through school RE classes and time in chapel) that the accident could have only happened because of something up there. I pursued it no further though. I didn't see the point of digging too deep.

After three years at school I was confirmed – it was, after all, the thing to do for a fourteen-year-old who attended a Church of England school. By the time I was entering my final year at school, aged sixteen, I was made head of chapel – not because of my religious beliefs, but probably because I had good organisational skills! Then after accepting the job I was told by some in my year that this was simply *the* un-coolest job around. I was mortified. The tears streamed from my eyes. I was uncool, or so I had been told. Perhaps that was one of the reasons I sat through chapel failing to pay attention to what was said, sung and prayed. It all passed over me, as I tried to regain any credibility I once had.

* * *

It wasn't until my first year at Newcastle University that I bumped into Julie again. I had met her about three years earlier when we were fifteen. Back then we used to meet outside a pub in Rock, in Cornwall, where we would drink cider, hang out with our mates, and generally cause a nuisance. Julie and I quickly fixed a time to meet for lunch so we could catch up. It had been a while since we had been together.

The following Tuesday we met up outside the students' union. Opposite was a big white tent. Students seemed to be pouring in and we were curious as to what it was all about. Then I realised – there was a big sign on the side of the tent saying, 'Free Lunch'! No wonder so many students were heading in that direction. One of the event organisers told us more about it, saying that after lunch there was going to be a brief talk about God. 'We've survived seven years of Christian stuff, one more "sermon" won't hurt us for the sake of a free lunch, will it?' I asked Julie. We headed towards the tent, not knowing that since I last saw Julie she had become a Christian. I wasn't going to turn down a free lunch, even if we had to listen to a Christian talk.

To say that the lunch was free it wasn't bad at all. While the cheese and pickle sandwiches looked a little dodgy, the ham baguettes tasted OK. Julie and I found our seats, the only ones left in the room, about halfway back from the front. It was all pretty relaxed. People carried on eating as the talk got going. I must admit I can't remember all of what was said, but I do remember that the speaker was talking about heaven and hell. It's fair to say, though, that I was interested. Growing up in a Muslim country such as Saudi Arabia, Christianity was something that was never taught. My only knowledge of Christianity was what I had received at secondary school in England. That was pretty basic however. I was keen to find out more about what Christians believed.

The man giving the talk showed obvious enthusiasm about Christianity; as he put it, 'Becoming a Christian has been the most exciting thing I have ever experienced.' He waved his arms around and gestured in all sorts of funny ways! If it was good enough for him, I was keen to find out if it was good enough for me. I filled in a response slip we were given on the way in. I ticked the box indicating my interest in a five-week course which would allow me to study the claims of Christianity in detail for myself.

* * *

That following week I attended the first evening of the Christianity Explored course. After a short talk we split up into groups to discuss the issues raised by the talk. Sometimes I would say quite a lot, surprising even myself, but other times I would claim ignorance telling them that I was not 'Christian enough' to comment.

My first real problem came when the topic of heaven and hell cropped up again. I could accept what the speaker had said at the lunchtime talk I attended the week before; that wasn't a problem. What he said appeared to be common sense. However, the discussion we were having now was a little less politically correct. I was told that the only way to heaven was through Jesus, i.e. by becoming a Christian. 'What about Mum and

Robbie?' I thought. I know they weren't Christians; was I now being told they were in hell? The thought of not seeing Robbie and my Mum again was enough for me to tell the group that I didn't want to become a Christian. I wasn't prepared to follow something, or someone, who would send my Mum and little brother to hell, when their lives were so tragically taken from them and from us.

I stuck the course out however, perhaps out of politeness, or perhaps because I was still intrigued by Christianity. Either way I was there each week. I still found it interesting no matter how repulsive the idea of hell was to me. I even started to attend a couple of the Christian Union meetings held in my halls of residence. Julie had encouraged me to go, telling me that they may help me in my understanding of who God is, and how He works. Unfortunately the hall group met on a Wednesday night – a massive student night in town. My loyalties were divided. I couldn't let go of the things that I was hearing at Christianity Explored though. One sentence from the Bible which we had read in the group was pounding in my mind. I couldn't ignore it. The sentence read: 'The curtain of the temple was torn in two from top to bottom.'[19] The sentence, I was told, symbolised the access that we now all have to God. The curtain was used to divide the temple, restricting the access people had to the most holy place. However, when Jesus came to this earth from heaven His sole purpose was to provide access to God, which had originally been restricted.

When Jesus died on the cross, I was told, He was creating a way back to God for every human. Each of us has done wrong and therefore each of us is separated from God. As He is perfect He cannot tolerate any wrong at all.

---

[19] Mark 15:38

Although I didn't want to admit it, I realised that I had done wrong, like everybody else. I knew I was cut off from God; I knew I had never known God; but I also knew that to know God must be absolutely amazing. I hoped that one day soon I would come to know Him for myself. Although I found it hard to reconcile a loving God with what had happened to my Mum and Robbie, I felt that what I was being told was worth considering. Besides, I felt as though I was running on empty. Perhaps Christianity did have some of the answers after all.

* * *

Term ended for the summer holidays and I returned home. The lazy summer days in London gave me more time to think. I began reading a book which I had been given years earlier by a family friend. It was called *Reaching for the Invisible God* by a man called Philip Yancey.[20] It talked about the reasons why we can trust and believe in God. It bombarded me with hard facts from the Bible. Each page I read made it harder and harder for me to escape the message of the Bible. It was compelling reading. But **it was more than a page turner; it was an eye-opener as to what Christians believe and why they have such confidence in it.**

Before long, Julie and I started meeting up on a weekly basis to read the Bible together. I was at a spiritual crossroads in my life. Which way would I choose to turn though?

My diary entry following our meeting that week read:

---

[20] Philip Yancey, *Reaching for the Invisible God: What Can We Expect to Find?* (Grand Rapids: Zondervan, 1994)

I'm scared that by learning about how to live from the Bible I am distancing myself from so many people. I know that there is a bigger picture to look at – eternity, but I can't help thinking 'why shouldn't I live in ignorance like other people?' I still have nightmares about Mum and Robbie... I'm happy when I'm with Christians because we all share in the same beliefs, so maybe the reason that I'm not as happy among my non-Christian friends is because I seem to be standing on my own. I realise that others feel like this too, but the example in the Bible shows me that by having faith in God I need not feel afraid.

I want to live for today and take tomorrow when I get there; that's not to say that I can't live happily as a Christian. It's just that in putting all this effort into the future I don't know whether I'm enjoying today. I know that God is to be seen as our Father. Like my Dad He may be unhappy with me for a while when I do wrong, but ultimately He still loves me. I find it helpful to make the comparison. My Dad gives rules and boundaries to live within and I need to obey them. When I make a mistake however and break them, He still loves me and wants to forgive me. The same is true with God – my heavenly father. I'm not sure why, but I feel that being forgiven by God is a much harder task. **Why do I feel like this? Why do I feel down?** Jesus died for my sins to be forgiven so I need not be down.

Now that I'm back home with friends – my really good friends – I sometimes feel out of place, feeling I know this truth, and concerned that they don't know God. I feel as though I have come so far into Christianity that I can't go back because I believe so much to be true. I'm not saying that I'd want to turn my back, I just want to know how to find peace of mind and peace of heart without hurting my friends, myself and God. I pray for these things and it's not like I feel that my prayers aren't being heard, it's only that I feel that there isn't actually an answer. I keep wondering: if the Bible is at the root of us, our foundations, then how can so many of us have ignored it? How can society be so sinful? I can't walk away now because I believe God to be true...

In the days that followed, and through many conversations with Julie later, I began to realise that my life had changed. My mind had been made up: Christianity was right. I *had* done wrong and I *did* need to be forgiven – just as the Bible said. I knew that I'd never known God; that I had been cut off from Him because of my sin. The only way back to Him was through Jesus and His death. There is a sentence in the Bible which says exactly that. It was Jesus who said: 'I am the way and the truth and the life. No-one comes to the Father except through me.'[21]

After I had asked Jesus to forgive me and come into my life, I began to live differently; to live as a Christian. There was still a pull on my life to live as most students do. The attraction of going into town and getting drunk was still there. But as a Christian, I am no longer living for myself and for my own desires, but I am living for God.

The subsequent weeks were a steep learning curve in my life as a Christian. I messed up and on occasions

---

[21] John 14:6

misunderstood what the Bible was teaching. However, with the help of my Christianity Explored leader I began learning more and more about God, His character, and the way He wanted me to live.

Even now, I'm still learning and still making mistakes. However, I can say with all my heart that I have found peace of mind and heart through the forgiveness, love, patience and guidance of a God who loved me enough to die for me, in my place, so that I may be reunited with Him. The hurt and pain of losing Mum and Robbie hasn't gone away, and I'm sure it never will. Nevertheless, **I now have a loving God by my side helping me when it's hardest. He has totally changed my life.**

Ville, Scandinavia

'It was the most humiliating experience of my life'

The thing that concerned Ville the most was to look good. As long as he kept up his image of being cool he was OK. Smoking had become a habit, pornography an addiction, and heavy drinking was now a routine. To many this wouldn't shock; however, Ville was only eleven years old.

Growing up in a small town of just over 6000 people meant that his actions were well publicised. What made things worse was that his parents were Christians. Ville was certainly not. Until about the age of nine he had held some form of religious belief, but looking back now he realises that this was merely a childlike acceptance of his parents' belief. Passing from childhood to teenage years, Ville soon left the religious beliefs behind, concerning himself only with whether he was cool or not. He was smoking like a chimney – often a packet a day, everyday. It came at a price. Ville and his friends would often have to wait around outside the convenience store until someone would go into the shop and buy them on their behalf. Of course, there would be a small mark-up price that would have to be paid. Ville's reputation was being bought at a significant price.

Finding others to buy their cigarettes was not always easy, leaving Ville and his friends with only one possible solution – stealing. Before long this became a habit. It was petty crime, but nevertheless it was becoming frequent. One afternoon, on his way home from school, the unthinkable happened. The manager of the small store at the end of Ville's road caught him stealing cigarettes. Fear swept over Ville's body as the manager called his parents. Thankfully for Ville, nobody was in. He and the manager struck up a deal. Ville would go home and tell his parents that he had been caught stealing. If the store manager received a phone call from Ville's parents before 5pm the police would not be called. However, if the phone didn't ring by then, Ville's school and the local police station would both be informed. For Ville it was the best option in a bad situation. When his mother returned home Ville confessed all.

'It was the most humiliating experience of my life', Ville remembers. *'My Mum was so disappointed with me. Her sadness was evident across her face. I felt that I had let her and my Dad down in a major way. I confessed to them the other thefts I had committed around the town, and that afternoon, I went to each of the stores, one by one, admitting what I had done, and paying them all back in full.'*

* * *

In Scandinavia church is a weekly event for most people. Even the irreligious would be found in church sometimes – following tradition, following the crowd. Most would attend the Lutheran Church. Ville's family were in the minority however, as they attended the small Pentecostal Church at the other end of the village. In doing so, they were setting themselves apart from everybody else. This led to a bitter resentment of Christianity and all that it stood for.

Whether Ville's desire to smoke and drink were driven by his aim to be cool or because he resented his parents' beliefs he is not sure. However, looking back he realises what a desperate time it was.

'I couldn't stop having nightmares. My life was spiralling out of control. I feared death terribly. *Heaven and hell were so vivid to me and I knew that because of the way I was living I deserved to go to hell. It was a terrifying thought, and one I couldn't escape. Even though I was ashamed of all the stuff I was doing, yet the ambition to be liked and accepted was too strong for me. I couldn't get out of the cycle I was in.'*

The existence of God plagued Ville's mind. Would he be punished for what he had done? Being brought up in a Christian family hadn't bothered Ville in some respects – he had loving parents and a stable home environment. Now however, Ville wished he knew nothing about Christianity. It was making him feel so guilty, remembering all that he had been taught as a child at church and at home. He knew what he was doing was wrong; he also knew that the voice of caution was not going to go away. He was continually reminded of all the wrong things he was doing; the wrong choices he was making – choices that even his friends would ridicule him about. But the grip of pornography and alcohol was too strong… he could never break free, could he?

Pornographic videos were not a possibility as his parents didn't own a television; the Internet was unavailable, which only left the option of dirty magazines. He had to be careful though, as his family would have been appalled to find such magazines in the house. At school however, Ville was open about his habit. He would admit to masturbating frequently, although his friends weren't too impressed. The memory of this time still haunts Ville. He remembers the taunting and bullying he received. But he had told them too much now. He couldn't turn back. He was addicted and he couldn't escape.

* * *

Ville began to look at his life. He felt so empty, so ashamed. He knew the way he was living was wrong. He knew it provided no future. He so desperately wanted to break free from it but he was trapped, or so he thought. Thoughts whirled around in his mind as he remembered all his parents had taught him about the Bible. He could vividly recall the pictures and illustrations that were used at Sunday school week after week; he knew the stories too. He'd been taught about how Jesus came to save people: those with no hope, who had rejected God and gone their own way. Ville could certainly identify with this. At twelve years old, he wasn't yet an adult and already his life was in a mess. As he came to realise, he had gone his own way.

'I couldn't avoid the persistent nagging going on in my head. I couldn't shake off the things I had heard at church. I had been taught clearly what the Bible said about those who rejected God. I knew that the Bible teaches that those who reject God will have to face the consequences of their decision. And those consequences are eternal. **I couldn't rest. My mind was active; I was afraid of facing God's judgment.** *I knew He was perfect, pure and lovely. The Bible describes His loving nature, His kindness, concern and compassion. I was disgusted at my own life, not just because of the things that I did, or looked at, but because my thoughts and attitudes were repulsive compared to the purity of God.'*

As time went by, Ville found it harder and harder to escape. Looking back now he realises that God was working in his life, exposing him for who he really was.

It frightened him. The one thing that comforted Ville most was the security he had in his own identity; however, this was now being tested. What could Ville be secure in now that God was exposing his helpless state?

* * *

Decision time arrived. It was now or never. Ville had to choose. He could either admit his guilt before Almighty God and live God's way, or live his own way, doing what he wanted but facing an empty future and the certainty of God's punishment upon him for all eternity.

For Ville the last few months had been turbulent, lonely and self-exposing. He was disgusted with his own life. He knew what he needed to do. He knew he needed to change, but he couldn't do it himself. Ironically, he feared telling his parents about what he was feeling, despite their faith in God. Sooner or later though, he knew he had to do it. He couldn't go on as he was.

On a late September afternoon, Ville made his way downstairs. He explained everything to his parents: the extent of his stealing; his addiction to drink; his smoking and the craving for pornography.

Tears ran down his mother's face – partly due to sadness at Ville's catalogue of confessions, but partly due to joy. Her son wanted to change! It was that afternoon that Ville confessed his sin to God pleading for His forgiveness.

> 'Dear God,' he prayed, 'I am sorry for all the wrong things that I've done. I've done some disgraceful things and have deliberately rejected obeying you. I know that you came to save people like me, people who have gone their own way. We cannot save ourselves, because the Bible explains that

nobody is right in your view. I need you to rescue me, forgive me, and change me. I want you to be in charge of my life. I don't want to do things my own way any more – I want to do them your way. I'm scared of telling my friends about this decision but I know that it's the right one. I know that if you are with me, even if my friends tease me, there is nothing I need to fear, but I need your help. I am trusting in you as my Lord and Saviour. Thank you for hearing this prayer. Amen.'

Ville felt humiliated and exposed as the message of Jesus uncovered the emptiness and worthlessness of his life. However, over a matter of weeks, it had brought him to a point of confession before God – a confession that was about to transform his whole life. Whilst he felt no radical difference – no physical changes, a peace began to settle in his mind and in his heart.

* * *

Ville returned to his gang of friends. They were the same as ever, and the pressure was on. Ville explained to the group what had happened, what he had prayed and why. This was the start of a lonely and friendless year and a half. They taunted him and mocked him for his previous 'hobby', pornography. They did their best to make sure a crowd was around when they did so, further ridiculing him. These 'friends' were rubbing his sin in his face and making him feel guilty for it; but Ville was not going to be knocked that easily. He knew that his decision had changed his life and changed his eternity. He was now at one with Almighty God: at peace with the creator of this universe who would one day be His Judge.

* * *

As is the custom with all males in Scandinavia, Ville was called up for military service. His faith was about to face another test. People mocked and teased, and the temptation to give up was immense. The physical challenge and exhaustion of his work was nothing compared to the spiritual challenge.

'Military training was as difficult as you would expect it to be. Physical ability was tested day after day after day. It was gruelling, leaving us feeling weak and unable to carry on. It was more than a physical test to me though. I was determined to prove that the decision I had made that September afternoon, in my living room, was not made on the spur of the moment, as an escape or crutch to the emptiness that I was feeling. The decision I made was permanent and I was determined to prove it.

*'You can imagine how the talk digresses when there are only guys around. As a Christian **I tried my best not to join in, but in my own way to live out the Christian message.** I made it clear that I was a Christian; for example, I didn't sleep with girls in my holidays. It has to be said that sometimes it was really difficult not to laugh at the jokes made, and not to join in with some of the conversations. I knew I couldn't survive using my own strength, because I had already seen where that would lead to. I needed God's strength, God's help and God's provision to see me through. He was more to me than I could ever have imagined. **The Bible teaches that God never leaves us or gives up on us and I can testify that this is true.'***

* * *

A few years later Ville moved across to the UK. He had responded to an advert he had seen on a notice board. He studied for his International Baccalaureate in Wales before a year or so later moving to Warwick to study for his degree. He recalls his time there.

'Life did not simply become easy just because I was a Christian. To be honest at times it can be hard. I'm now involved in the Christian Union at Warwick which is a great help and support to me as a Christian. I'm learning a lot about the Bible, which explains God's character, His beauty, and His desire for us to be like Him. I still mess up. I still have to battle with the temptation to return to what I was like before. But there have been a couple of sections in the Bible that have really stood out for me and helped me to carry on. This is what they say:

> And we know that God causes everything to work together for the good of those who love God and are called according to his purpose for them… And having chosen them, he called them to come to him. And he gave them right standing with himself, and he promised them his glory. What can we say about such wonderful things as these? If God is for us, who can ever be against us? Since God did not even spare his own Son but gave him up for us all, won't God, who gave us Christ, also give us everything else?
>
> Who dares accuse us whom God has chosen for his own? Will God? No! He is the one who has given us right standing with himself. Who then will condemn us? Will Christ Jesus? No, for he is the one who died for us and was raised to life for us and is sitting at the place of highest honour next to God, pleading for us.
>
> Can anything ever separate us from Christ's love? Does it mean he no longer loves us if we have trouble or calamity, or are persecuted, or are

hungry or cold or in danger or threatened with death?... No, despite all these things, overwhelming victory is ours through Christ, who loved us.

And I am convinced that nothing can ever separate us from his love. Death can't, and life can't. The angels can't, and the demons can't. Our fears for today, our worries about tomorrow, and even the powers of hell can't keep God's love away. Whether we are high above the sky or in the deepest ocean, nothing in all creation will ever be able to separate us from the love of God that is revealed in Christ Jesus our Lord.'[22]

Jesus said, 'Mark my words, no one who sacrifices house, brothers, sisters, mother, father, children, land – whatever – because of me and the Message will lose out. They'll get it all back, but multiplied many times in homes, brothers, sisters, mothers, children, and land – but also in troubles. And then the bonus of eternal life! This is once again the Great Reversal: Many who are first will end up last, and the last first."[23]

'Like with everyone, life can still be hard, but I know that God is with me. He keeps His promises and He has promised that one day I will be with Him in heaven forever – and that beats anything this world can offer. Nothing compares to having a real and lasting friendship with Almighty God and I am so glad I am His and He is mine.'

---

[22] Romans 8:28,30–35,37–39 (NLT)
[23] Mark 10:29–31 (The Message)

If Ville's story has raised some difficult issues for you and you would find it helpful to talk with someone confidentially, please contact Friends International:

Tel: +44 (0)20 8780 3511
Email: info@new2uk.org

Tom, Ireland/France

'My degree was my god'

Religion was a way of life to me. I grew up with it really. My father, who came from the very south of Ireland, was brought up as a devout Roman Catholic. My mother, who was French, had also been brought up with the same beliefs. Growing up in France I saw many of my friends conform to this way of life. If someone had asked me back then, I would have said that Christianity and Catholicism were the same thing.[24] It was all about being a good person, or at least that's what it seemed. 'Everyone *knows* one should be a good person...I don't need to go to church to be told this,' I reasoned. Anyway, I was doing fine by myself; I didn't need any religion to make me a better person.

When I arrived at Durham University to study law my religion was one of the first things that I left behind. Although it had never really been a major part of my life in France, it had been hard to escape. Now, I was free from all that, and I was going to make sure I had a wild

---

[24] For further reading on this issue see Dwight Longenecker and John Martin, *Challenging Catholics* (Carlisle: Paternoster Press, 2001)

time at university. **Attending church was never a question – I never intended to go.**

My first year at Durham was a blur of free living. I played lots of sport, drank huge amounts of alcohol, flirted with girls, and occasionally went to a lecture. There were some Christians in my college who seemed nice enough. However, they did say some slightly weird things, like 'I love Jesus' and 'I have a relationship with God.' I remember thinking to myself how embarrassing this was. 'Normal, sensible students cannot go around saying they love Jesus. It's not right!' I thought I could help these Christians to see the light – to see that being a Christian was just a crutch for the weak. They were vulnerable people who needed someone like me to put them right.

* * *

That first year at university went so quickly. I scraped through my first-year law exams with a 49 percent average – not what I was hoping for. My law professor told me to expect a low second-class degree with marks like those. 'Well, I didn't come to university to get that,' I thought to myself.

Returning for my second year work became my life. Hours of study in the library became routine. No longer would I lie in bed past noon. Noon meant lunchtime now, not breakfast! What was driving me to work so insanely hard was the fear of failure. I didn't come to university to fail; therefore I wasn't going to. It was as simple as that. This new work commitment didn't rule out the party lifestyle all together though. The late nights, the drinking, and the chasing girls remained part of my life, but now it was just in the evenings rather than all day.

Life looked great to the onlooker. My grades were improving, I was in the sports teams and I was certainly having a great time at evenings and weekends. To those around me life was going smoothly. **Inside however, I was in a mess.** I had had two relationships with good friends of mine. Both were lovely girls, though through my own fault the relationships ended horribly. I was utterly selfish in my attitude towards them; I even shocked myself at the way I had acted. Clearly, I was not the good moral guy I thought I was. It was worse than just one mistake. This was the way I was, and for all my efforts in changing I couldn't alter what I was really like deep down. My actions were dreadful and the feelings that came with it were getting me down.

I was living with some Christians in my second year (though not by choice). I had made it clear at the start of the year that they were not to try and convert me. I was certainly not going to be forced into Christianity. Following the break-up of my two relationships, one of my flatmates was a really good friend to me. She invited me to a couple of lunchtime talks that the Christian Union had organised. I'm not sure why, but I went along. The Christians actually seemed quite nice. This surprised me! They were different for some reason – they had a security and confidence from something, but I couldn't understand what. There was no-one more successful than me. In fact, without being arrogant, I was probably more successful than they were; yet they were so much happier. I was confused.

I was intrigued. I wanted to understand what it was that made these people so different. Many things changed over the next few months: I went to talks that the Christian Union were doing and began to attend a small group meeting where we studied the Bible together. I even went to a mission week. Organised by the Christian Union, the aim was to encourage people to get to know more about Jesus. It was weird – eighteen months before, I wouldn't have dreamed of going anywhere near a

Christian meeting; yet now, I was attending every Christian meeting I could to try and understand the security that these people had.

Deep down I desperately wanted the peace that they had, but I really couldn't accept their beliefs for what they were. It baffled me that intelligent people could believe what I considered to be a child's fairy story. How could they believe that the world was created in seven days? Why did they think that this man Jesus was actually God? And where did they get the idea that God was somehow three people? Going to the talks and Bible studies I had decided to ask the hardest questions I could.[25] I wanted to prove that Christianity didn't stand up when tested. I thought that **somebody needed to wake these people up; I would do it by asking one hard question after another.**

First, I tried questioning Jesus' identity. 'How can you believe that Jesus is the Son of God?' I asked. 'Surely He is a man from history, a man with a big beard and sandals, but you Christians have made Him into something He is not.' My second point of attack was the Bible: 'How can you believe that the Bible is the Word of God? It is written in the same ink as any other book, on the same paper as any other book, and it sits on the same shelf as other books – but you're telling me this is a divine book?' Though I asked the toughest questions I could think of there were always answers, and to my surprise, the answers were *really* good! They were reasonable and valid.

They explained that the documents supporting the gospels, the four books of the Bible which tell us most about Jesus' life, are extremely reliable in terms of ancient

---

[25] For a more in-depth look at some of these issues see Josh McDowell and Don Stewart, *Answers to Tough Questions* (Milton Keynes: Authentic Media, 2006)

history. In fact, the Bible was uniquely attested in terms of ancient historical documentation. Further, there was strong support from non-Christian historians, as well as archaeological evidence. I struggled to argue with this. Neither could I explain how the Bible, made up of 66 books and written over 1,600 years by over 40 different authors – many of whom had never heard of each other – could have such unity of purpose, theme and expression. I began to see that the Bible from beginning to end was the unfolding story of God's plan for salvation. I began to realise that this book that they called the Bible was indeed special and worth exploring further.[26]

* * *

I spent around six months looking into the evidence of the Christian message and whether it was relevant to me. I came to the conclusion that quite possibly Christianity was real and true. However, I had a problem – I didn't want to become a Christian. Although I wanted my conscience cleared of the wrong things I had done I didn't want to change my lifestyle. My Christian friends, including my flatmate, explained that becoming a Christian was more than a one-off commitment. It involved a lifestyle change. For someone who liked to party this wasn't what I wanted to hear. All I wanted was to carry on as I was without the feeling of guilt that so often riddled my mind.

For the next ten months I tried not to think about Christianity. I dismissed it from my mind, pretending and wishing I had never asked any questions in the first place. I wished I could have blocked out those times of

---

[26] For a further explanation about the Bible see Henrietta Mears, *What the Bible is All About* (California: Regal Books, 1995)

exploring the Christian faith. Anyway, I now had more important things to think about... the dreaded summer exams! Forty-nine percent for my first-year exams was not acceptable. The pressure was on to improve on last year's result.

Thankfully, the exams went well. When the marks came back a few weeks later, my first year exam result was just a distant memory. I could now add academic achievement to my list of successes. Once again, I was flying high, and life was good. Well, perhaps not really good, but at least I had passed!

* * *

Third year was going to be different from second year. My degree was my god, but even good results didn't fill the void that I had deep down. So instead I tried making other things the centre of my life. Rowing, running, rugby, basketball – I would try my hand at any sport on offer, whether for the university, the college teams or just for fun. It didn't fill the gaping hole inside me though – an emptiness which gripped my life so tightly that it was choking everything that I was relying on for happiness. I only knew one more thing that I could try... partying!

I partied as hard as I could. From drinking games to casual relationships I was at the centre of it all. I was always the first in the queue at the bar – and frequently the last one crawling to bed after a particularly heavy night of drinking. Looking back now, it's no surprise that the intense drinking habits which left me staggering back along the streets of Durham didn't fill the empty void in my life.

I went back to France at Christmas, struggling to know what to do. The unrest in my mind wasn't being answered, and I wasn't sure where else to look. Well, that is, apart from one place. Yes, I allowed my mind to consider Christianity once again.

* * *

Midway through the Easter term a friend of mine from the Bible study group I used to go to asked to meet me for a coffee. Jason said he was paying, and being a student, I was not going to say no. He had become quite a good friend and I respected him, so it was good to meet up. I knew that Christianity was going to be a topic of conversation, but I had never imagined that he would say what he did. I will never forget it.

'Tom, I'm really worried about you.'

I was shocked. How did he know that things weren't great?

'I'm worried you're going to leave university without deciding who Jesus really is,' he finished.

I didn't know what to think. Christianity might have seemed like a point of academic historical interest, but now I wasn't so sure. I couldn't understand how it mattered to me at that moment. What I could see however was how important it was to him. Jason was not messing around. His face was serious and his tone was solemn. I recognised how brave he had been in saying what he had said. He had risked being on the receiving end of my bad temper, which I had become known for. His words were heartfelt. They had a profound impact upon me.

Although our conversation that day bowled me over, it failed to mark a huge change in my life. In many ways things continued as normal. Looking back, however, this was the start of a life-changing process. I began to meet with Jason to study the Bible. Tentatively I started considering Christianity once more. He took me to a book in the Bible called Romans, written by the Apostle Paul. Week by week, as we looked more closely at what was being said, my own sin was becoming more and more obvious. Paul wrote about how our sin stops us having a relationship with God. In fact he tells us that because of our wrongdoing we are cut off and condemned before God. Jason pointed out the sentence which begins, 'all have sinned and fall short of the glory of God...'[27] I didn't need to be told that I had done wrong. I realised that however hard I might try to be a good person, I couldn't be good enough. My sins might not hit the headlines or put me in prison, but I had consistently neglected God and put myself first. I was an utterly selfish person, and my only hope was to limit the damage, nothing more. Or so I thought.

I still didn't want to become a Christian. For me, becoming a Christian was like becoming a monk – replacing fun and spontaneity with solemn and serious looks, trying to forget about all those things you could no longer do. **I was still struggling to understand that being a Christian was about having a relationship with God rather than being all about rules and regulations.**

During my next holiday I read two very helpful Christian books, and spent a lot of time talking with a Christian friend of mine; once again I was asking lots of tough questions. One of the books I read was about the rationality of Christianity.[28] I was impressed by how intellectually robust Christianity actually was. I began to realise that to be a Christian did not require switching off your brain. The other book I read was very different. It told the story of a twenty-year-old

---

[27] Romans 3:23
[28] C.S. Lewis, *Mere Christianity* (London: HarperCollins, 2001)

whose life was dramatically changed after becoming a Christian.[29]

Through reading this I saw how Jesus changes lives. He turns them upside down and radically alters them for the better. I began to see how becoming a Christian was about entering into a dynamic and exciting relationship with God, through Jesus. I saw, once again, that being a Christian was more than a one-off decision; it affected every part of your life. I was still unsure though whether this was for me or not. I wanted to change, but I wasn't sure whether I wanted to make such a big commitment.

* * *

It was the final stretch – the last term. I had arrived a week before the start of term which, although unplanned, gave me time to think through some of the major issues concerning Christianity.

I remember the night well. It was a cool, cloudless evening on that Sunday night, the 27th of April. I had just come back from the college bar and was talking to my flatmate when it hit me: 'If what Jesus did was true, then I *could have* everything I could possibly want in the world right now. I didn't need anything more but Jesus.' It was an incredible moment. **All the pieces of the jigsaw suddenly fitted together.** For the first time I realised that when Jesus, the Son of God, died on the cross He took the punishment that I deserved. He was carrying my sins upon Himself. He died in my place. In that moment, a tremendous weight was lifted off my shoulders. For the past 18 months I had been so convicted of my guilt and had struggled in trying to deal with it

[29] Melody Green and David Hazard, *No Compromise* (Oregon: Harvest House, 2000)

myself. So there and then, in the midst of an untidy bedroom, I prayed to God, asking for His forgiveness. I asked that He would remove my sin and change me. It was as though I had been handcuffed to my sins but now I was free – through Jesus, all my wrong had been paid for. It was an emotional moment… an amazing moment! But then someone walked into the room and the emotions disappeared. I didn't know what to think. Was the moment gone? Was I still forgiven? Was I now a Christian or had it been a temporary emotional moment? What was happening?

I went back to my room later that evening and began to pray:

> 'God, if you're there please will you show yourself to me? I know I've never really believed in you before but I want to now. I want to live for you.'

I prayed and prayed. I read the Bible until eventually my eyes became weary and I fell asleep.

The next morning I woke up feeling terrible. 'If this is what the Christian life is like,' I remember thinking, 'then I'm not a big fan.' I felt awful. I couldn't stop thinking about what Christianity meant. It was consuming my mind, and in just six weeks I would be sitting my final law exams.

I packed my rucksack before making the short walk across to the Law library. But I couldn't concentrate. I couldn't help thinking about Jesus. Did He hear my prayer? If so, was He going to answer me?

Packing my books up for the second time that day, I left the library and headed for home. But I was side-tracked by the grand building next to the library, the Cathedral. I found a seat near the back which was away from any distractions or interruptions, and I began to pray. I asked God to tell me if I was a Christian. I really wasn't sure.

It was then that a conversation I had two years ago with a friend came to mind. We had talked about the Columbine high school shootings in America. During the shootings one of the gunmen challenged a girl named Cassie and asked 'Do you believe in God?' 'Yes,' she had replied confidently, even though she knew this would lead to her being shot by the gunman. My friend had said that she would have done the same. I was so annoyed at the time. I simply couldn't believe that an intelligent person would say that. I had responded, 'You should just say, "No I don't believe in God", and they would let you live. Yes, you've told a lie, but the important thing is that you're still alive.' I was really angry and offended that she could have answered so stupidly.

But, leaving the Cathedral that day, I realised that without doubt or hesitation I would now say 'Yes' in that situation, because I knew that having trusted in Jesus I was going to heaven. All the evidence I had looked at: the reliability of the Bible under tough questioning; the proof of who Jesus was; the accuracy with which the Bible spoke of my life; the evidence of lives changed in Christians around me... all of these came together.

I finally did it. I accepted the weight of the evidence. Jesus *really* did die on the cross, and in doing so carried my sin, and the sins of the world on Himself. He truly did come back to life three days after His death, and so opened the way to eternal life through Him, and only Him! This was no longer a historical question, but a hugely personal truth. I realised the sacrifice of Jesus' death on the cross was so huge that it demanded me to change, to turn away from my life of selfish living and to live for God; not that this could make me acceptable to God by itself, but that it might simply be my humble thank you to God for His astounding gift of eternal life with Him! A new life, through His help, living for God.

Tom recently graduated from Durham University and has plans to one day go back to France. However, becoming a Christian doesn't mean that life suddenly becomes easy as Tom explains.

'There have been plenty of challenges in my life since becoming a Christian. True, Christianity is not a denial of the reality of this difficult world – as Christians we still live in the same troubled world as everybody else. However, we have a Saviour in Jesus, and a constant companion. There have been some difficult times for me since that day in the Cathedral but God has been there for me ever since. I can honestly say that He is faithful to His promise of working things out for good, for those who love Him.

'Since becoming a Christian, I have enjoyed my life so much more than before. In the Bible Jesus said, "I have come that you might have life, and have it to the full."[30] I can testify to this being true – in Jesus lies the fullness of life itself. The intimacy and depth to a relationship with God is brilliant. The day I became a Christian was and still is the best one of my life. Nothing can beat having your sins forgiven, your guilt removed, and a lasting, personal relationship with the Creator of the world.'

---

[30] John 10:10

Ivy, China

'I thought I was OK as I was'

To be honest, it wasn't traumatic leaving China to study in a foreign land. I grew up in Shangai, the biggest and the busiest city in China. Everywhere you look, whether during the day, or late at night, people crowd the streets. From business people to everyday shoppers, Shanghai is China's equivalent of New York. I was used to the hustle and bustle of living in a place where you can get almost anything you want. On top of that, I had had the privilege of being able to travel to most of the major countries in Eastern Europe. So when I arrived at my hall of residence in a rain sodden Headingley, on the outskirts of Leeds, England, I had little fear of what I might face. It was all an adventure to me.

Despite the size of the two cities, I thought there was little difference between Shanghai and Leeds. It wasn't until I had been in Leeds a few weeks that I felt one major difference – freedom of speech. At home there isn't the freedom to say what we like on the television, radio, or in public places. However, as I listened to the radio, or turned on the television I was shocked at the freedom that people had here in expressing their feelings and opinions so openly.

There is just one other slight difference too – there are churches that people can attend. In China **I had had little or no exposure to religion.** The only contact I had had was with my father's boss, Timothy. Despite being his boss, he was also my father's close friend. Timothy would often come round to our house for meals and became close to the whole of the family. I always referred to him as Uncle Timothy; for some reason that felt more appropriate.

Uncle Timothy was also a Christian. However, despite Timothy's strong beliefs, my mother and father had never given Christianity – or any religion for that matter – much thought. Only when I left for university in England did they allow me to investigate Christianity further; as for it ever making an impact upon their own lives, it never had.

* * *

Uncle Timothy accompanied my parents to the airport as they waved me off. After the last hug goodbye had been given, moments before boarding the plane, Uncle Timothy placed something in my hand. It was a Chinese Bible. As he did so he hugged me again, saying, 'You should read this while you're away. I can assure you it will give you a true peace and joy in your heart.'

Uncle Timothy always said this sort of thing. Whenever he had the opportunity, he would tell us about how 'Jesus had changed his life; how He had given Him a lasting happiness in his heart – no matter what circumstances he faced.' I never really knew what to make of everything that he told us. I guess I thought it was great for him, but that I was OK as I was. One thing I couldn't escape though was the fact he always seemed happy. It was slightly unnerving.

* * *

Leaving China wasn't a worry for me. But as I unpacked my bag, and decorated my room with things from home, I began to think just how far away China was. It made me feel homesick. So I decided that I was going to join in with as many activities as possible, in the hope that I would make lots of new friends. By making friends, I thought, I would soon get over the feeling of missing home.

There was so much happening that I could get involved in. International Freshers' Week was a busy week and I tried to do as much as possible. I wandered around the stalls with information about the different clubs and societies. One society that interested me was the Christian Union. They had a big tent in the centre of the university with a coffee shop inside. I went in and chatted to a couple of people while drinking some English tea for the first time. They told me all about the programme of events they had planned for the week, and also mentioned the regular activities during term time.

The people from the Christian Union were like Uncle Timothy: ever so friendly, very kind, and their smiles were just as big as his! I spent a lot of time with them and they were good to me, helping me out with the language, as well as telling me things that I would need to know about Leeds. I wasn't bothered that they were religious, as I didn't really think it would affect me. They were nice people, and I thought that by spending time with them I could learn a lot about the culture in England, which would really help me settle in.

That's what I thought when one of my friends invited me along to church. Of course I agreed to go, not thinking too much about the fact that I was going to church; I was going for the cultural experience, not for a religious one.

I sat listening and watching all that went on. It was interesting to see what they did. As my friend and I made our way home for lunch I couldn't help but think how happy everyone at church had been; just like my Uncle Timothy – but I didn't know why. I couldn't understand what made Christians so happy about everything.

After spending time with friends from the Christian Union over the next couple of weeks, I was intrigued. **My interest was more than cultural** for I had seen how Christianity had also impacted Uncle Timothy's life; **I wanted to know what it was that was affecting these people so much.** It was positive; it was something that made these people likeable, and that wasn't something I could say about everyone at university.

* * *

It was later that week that I was invited to a course run by the Christian Union. It took place every week for six weeks. They called it 'An Introduction to Jesus and the Bible.' It sounded like just the thing I needed. I had so many questions that I wasn't sure where to start. I thought that attending this course might help me find some answers. It might explain why Christians were so different.

The course was excellent. There was always plenty of English food to eat, and the people leading the group were very thoughtful in how they explained things about the Bible. Knowing that the group consisted of people from all over the world with English as their second or third language, they had thought through simple ways to explain what the Bible said. I remember one of them using pictures to explain who Jesus was and what He did, which helped me a lot.

I still had lots of questions though. Is there life after death? Is there a reason we are here? And why are there so many problems in this world; God could surely do something about them? I had read in the Bible that Uncle Timothy gave me, that we should have love, joy, peace, patience, and that we should be kind, good, faithful, gentle and self-controlled – but I thought this seemed impossible. I couldn't understand how we could do all these things. If God was in control of us, why didn't we live up to his expectations?

* * *

By the time the six-week course had nearly ended, I was regularly attending church. I had been every week for nearly two months by now. Again, the people there were really thoughtful, remembering that English wasn't my first language. They tried to speak slowly, so that I could understand them. We would laugh together at my mistakes, as they corrected me, and put my words in the right order. They were always so kind, and so good at putting me at ease.

One week I sat next to a lawyer. I had seen him at church before, and had spoken to him a couple of times. His name was James. We chatted for a while and I told him I had read a few parts of the Bible. He looked impressed! But I explained that I still had a lot of questions.

'Why don't you ask me some?' he said.

I felt a little silly, but thought I would ask him anyway. One after another he carefully but clearly explained to me how the Bible answers my questions.

For example, he explained why Jesus was born as a baby into this world. James told me that Jesus came to earth because we needed to be rescued from the punishment we deserve for rejecting God and going our own way. The way He could rescue us was by being punished for us – taking what we deserve. He was the only person that could do this, because He was totally perfect. So, Jesus, God's Son, lived a perfect life, and faced God's punishment while dying on a cross, so that we might not have to face the punishment we deserve.

'This is what gives us real meaning to life – when we thank God for all He has done for us and accept His free gift of forgiveness and life with Him as our God. When we do that He promises that He will help us to become more and more like Him in our character, until one day, when we die, or He brings the world to an end, we will go to heaven and live forever. And there will be no pain or tears or suffering in heaven; it will be a perfect place which we will enjoy forever.'

We talked for a long time and then James prayed for me. Afterwards, I remember him asking me whether I wanted to ask Jesus to rescue and save me from the punishment I deserved; if I wanted to become a Christian. It must have been written on my face, because that is exactly what I wanted to do! He had so clearly explained what Jesus had done for me that I knew that is what I had to do. I still had unanswered questions about a few things, but I knew enough to know that I wanted what James and my other Christian friends had: peace with God which comes through forgiveness from Him.

So that morning, with James as my witness, I asked Jesus to be my Saviour. I asked Him to be in control of my life, to be my Lord and Saviour.

* * *

The peace and joy that Uncle Timothy had talked about is now mine. Becoming a Christian has changed me dramatically. **I still have questions and struggles,**

but the bottom line is always what Jesus has done for me. I may not understand everything about God, but what I do know is that He has made it possible for me to be forgiven and for me to be one of His children. No unanswered question can ever change that. Over time, I have slowly changed, just as the Bible says, to become more and more like God. I still do things wrong, which God hates, but because of Jesus I am forgiven. As the Bible says, the blood of Jesus, God's Son, cleanses us from all sin.[31]

* * *

Not only has becoming a Christian changed Ivy's life, but it is also having an effect on the life of her family, as she explains.

'My parents are really pleased to know about the peace that following Jesus has brought me. My Dad's now interested in Christianity as well, and I hope that when I'm home I'll be able to tell him all about it. My Mum doesn't have any particular thoughts on religion, but doesn't really want to interfere with my beliefs as long as I still work hard and get a good result in my academic studies. I find it even harder to tell my friends about Jesus, and all that's happened to me. I always tell them about my Christian life in Leeds, but they seem more interested in my academic and social life than what I am involved in as a Christian.

'I wouldn't change anything though, regardless of what my friends say or think. I am so happy to know that God loves me; that He has forgiven me by dying for me, and that now I'm living as He wants me to.

'Since I became a Christian, I have a deep understanding about love, joy and peace. In loving our neighbour as

---

[31] See 1 John 1:7

Christ loves us we are living in God's holy way not in our own sinful way. It does not earn me any more love or reward from God, however, He is pleased when we do as He has commanded. It is amazing that we cannot be loved anymore by God: He already loves us completely. But because of all He has done for us, it is right that we should live for Him.

'Jesus' death has been something I have come back to many times – it was the basis of many of my questions and struggles. I do have a peace in my heart even when I struggle with problems. Jesus' death makes me realise that He has already taken the punishment that I really deserve. And His resurrection reminds me that death has been conquered. I will never be afraid or without hope for God is always with me, forever and ever. When I die, I know that I will go to be with Him in heaven. Nothing in the world can ever be better than that.'

Ivy has one year left at Leeds University, after which she plans to apply to study for a Masters. She hopes that one day she will return to work in her home country.

Matt, India

*'I couldn't maintain the double life
I was leading'*

I was given my first Bible at seven years old. The smell of
incense and spice lifted as I flicked through the pages of
a book rich in history. I was excited and enthralled by the
mysteries inside. Wise old priests with their white
flowing beards had entrusted me with the sacred book –
or so I thought – and I would not let them down.

I grew up in the bustling and sprawling city of New
Delhi. We lived in an exclusive part of the city, home to
government officials and Foreign Service personnel. My
mother was an extremely talented and energetic lady
who had done well in her career as a diplomat and might
soon be an ambassador. Her parents were both army
doctors and so her family had spent a lot of time on the
move, mainly in Burma (southeastern Asia) and India.
My father, on the other hand, belonged to a large, close
knit and traditional Malayali family from the same
village as my mother. My parents' marriage had been
arranged by my grandparents, as is still the custom in
India today. Soon after their marriage my parents moved
to Delhi where my sister was born, and then on to
London where I was born. When my mother was posted

back to India my father remained in England to complete his training as a doctor.

* * *

Memories of my early years in India are vague and nostalgic. My sister and I would accompany my mother to diplomatic functions, which were full of elaborate ceremony. We used to enjoy meeting people from different lands, marvelling at their strange dresses and stranger customs. We would look on proudly at my mother who could converse effortlessly with them all, often in their own language. My mother's particular passion was to build cultural understanding between India and other countries.

On summer holidays we would take the three-day train journey from Delhi to Trivandrum in the South, staying with my mother's parents. Grandfather was a gentle and kind man with a big laugh; he was enjoying retirement. Grandmother was a few years younger than him and was still busy delivering babies in the local hospital. The evenings were spent relaxing on the veranda or in their large and airy sitting room, with the noise of crickets or tiny lizards providing background music, and the strip neon lights flickering as the evening power cut took place. In the evenings there was the regular routine of listening to the BBC World Service on radio, followed by a Bible reading and prayer time – all before we went to bed. On Sundays we would go to the Syrian Orthodox Church. Powdered ladies in their beautifully bright saris and men in their spotless white *dhotis* and *jubbahs* thronged through its richly decorated teak doors. Inside, the whole congregation chanted prayers in Malayalam and Syriac, the words entwining with the incense and ceremony. It seemed as if the whole village was at church.

The services were long and my mind would soon wander, longing for the final prayer to be said. The ceremony of the service bored me; **all I wanted to do was reach for the Bible and find out more about this mysterious book.** After church we would go to the cemetery where prayers were said for the departed in my family. It seemed to me these holidays were full of adventure, new friendships, and, most importantly, Malayali delicacies – fried bananas, fried fish or plantain chips. Before long though, the end of the summer arrived and it meant it was time to return. A long, hot and sticky train journey took us home, back to the capital and back to school.

By the age of four I was attending a private school in New Delhi. It was run by Irish Catholic priests, who combined a sincere faith with strict discipline. Catholic Mass was taken every day as part of our school assembly. My sister studied in the girls' school opposite mine. A large, ornate, Catholic Church building separated the two. On Sundays we would attend the local Anglican Church together as well, where many expatriates worshipped.

During these years my parents had been living apart, as already mentioned. Their relationship had been under a lot of strain over the years and this was beginning to appear. My mother's chances of another posting in London were remote, so she decided to take an extended leave of absence from the Foreign Service and join my father in England. I was excited yet afraid. It was in 1979 that my mother and I landed in Heathrow, leaving my sister behind at boarding school in India. My father greeted us at the airport, and as he kissed me and embraced my mother, my fear melted away. My sister joined us a year later and my mother subsequently resigned from her post in the Foreign Service.

* * *

Over the next two years we moved a lot between hospitals as my father pursued his career. The doctors' flats were filled with families from all over the world and I soon became an expert in making friends and then saying goodbye as people moved on. My father would often be out late in the evening at the hospital so it was my mother who always put us to bed. Every night she would pray with my sister and me. My main recurring prayer was for the safety of my family. I imagined fierce and violent people waiting around every street corner, determined to remove us to our homeland. My Bible was always tucked under my pillow as ultimate protection in case my prayers hadn't reached God.

At weekends when my father wasn't working we all went into the heart of London to attend the Orthodox Church service. The same prayers were chanted and the same incense was burned. We always arrived late but no one seemed to mind. Everyone knew my family, and the church provided all of us with a much needed sense of belonging and a continued link with India. However, God continued to be an abstract idea, having no particular influence on my life except that I believed in His kindness.

In 1980 Luis Palau, a well-known evangelist from South America, put on a series of meetings in London. I can't remember what he spoke about, but I remember that the football stadium was full and that people sang and listened intently to what was being said. Thousands – my sister included – were moved enough to respond to the invitation to collect more information about Christianity after the meeting. I was just happy that I had finally got to sit in a real football stadium!

Four years later, my father took up a permanent position in Northern Ireland. Although family, friends and neighbours in England were worried for our safety, we all were glad that this job finally meant stability. There would be no more moving and no more job insecurity for my father. We settled in a seaside town – as far away as you could imagine from the newspaper reports of violence in Northern Ireland that shocked the nation on a daily basis. I attended a boys' grammar school and, being one of only two non-Irish boys in my year, was obviously different. However, the Irish were warm and friendly. My peers accepted me, in spite of my different accent.

My father immersed himself in his work and would relax by spending hours in the garden while my mother busied herself in the home. She was the one I would confide in. I was hard working at school and loved sport. Sundays became another day to play tennis or meet up with friends. I continued to faithfully tuck my Bible under my pillow, but that was the extent of my religion. I assumed everyone at school was a Christian. The Christian Union, however, was poorly attended and was, I thought, only for people who had nothing else to do in their lunch break. By contrast I had tennis, hockey, cricket, chess, exams, alcohol, cigarettes and girls to keep me busy. The only other Asian in my school was a close friend who had, in his words, been 'born again' as a Christian. I remember an extremely heated debate with him when I tried to argue against his claim that Jesus was the only way to God, and that everyone else would be going to hell. I found this offensive and couldn't believe my friend could think that way. I challenged him about people who had never heard of Jesus – those who were mentally disabled or those who had died in their mother's womb. 'What happens to them?' I asked.

* * *

My mother had become increasingly dissatisfied with staying at home. She applied for a senior position in a voluntary organisation and was appointed, which in turn generated a lot of interest and attention in the local media. One year into her post she had her first mental breakdown. **It was unexpected and totally devastating. I thought she was invincible; she had always been the anchor in my life, keeping me steady.** Now all this was gone. Over the next three years my mother went in and out of hospital. I became increasingly self-reliant and was unwilling to share any of my pain with anyone, including my father.

My sister had moved to university and for the first time I felt alone. Friends could not offer any help; they didn't know of my inner turmoil. I think I was secretly ashamed of what I perceived was my family's disgrace. My only salvation was school and sport during the week; at the weekend alcohol and nightclubs were my ways of escape.

During this period a Christian couple befriended my family. They had worked as missionaries in India for a number of years and still had an obvious love and concern for its people. They had been introduced to my parents through my friendship with my Christian friend at school. They used to visit or phone on a regular basis, and over time I came to know them and love them. They were so different from many other Christians I had met; they knew what the Bible said, prayed with us and were sacrificial in their love.

* * *

At the age of eighteen I moved to university. The first few months flew by. I had my own flat and complete freedom! It seemed that **university life was all about going out with your friends and getting drunk.** The more drunk you were the funnier the things you might do – which meant that you had more to boast about the next day. That was until the first major exam arrived. Failure meant re-sits and the possibility of losing my place at medical school. I decided to go temporarily into halls of residence – into self-imposed exile – and do some work.

The accommodation was dreadful. The halls were situated in one of the most deprived areas of Belfast. The only positive feature was that it smelled like an Indo-Chinese restaurant! They were full of students from abroad who found comfort in talking in their own languages, growing their own chillies and cooking their own exotic dishes. Among them were a few Christians. Being obsessed with food I soon thought of starting a dinner-time rota. Soon we had fourteen enlisted, and we had teams of two preparing delicious meals at very low prices. My speciality was cow heart curry – serves thirteen for £4.50!

These were great opportunities to spend time together. I remember the talk turning to religion. Around the table was a mixture of Buddhists, Atheists, Hindus, Christians and Muslims. When a Christian friend asked me whether I had a relationship with God, I was immediately challenged. I had always thought that God was abstract, but in the pressure of the moment I replied yes. I knew I didn't; I wasn't even aware that God wanted a relationship with me.

Over the next year, as the question penetrated deeper into my soul, I became increasingly troubled. During this time friends used to meet for Bible study and prayer. The lives of many in this group were an inspiration, including the Chinese-Malaysian friend who had asked me the question about my relationship with God. Five years before he had been deeply depressed and suicidal. Something had changed him, and it wasn't temporary. He radiated love and peace. There was the same sense of blessing in his life that I saw in the Christian missionary couple from home. Their prayers and life were evidence that they had a relationship with this Jesus.

Exams loomed and I pushed thoughts of God to the back of my mind. Through a lot of prayer from friends and long nights of study I managed to claw my way through the exams. The next few months were spent in the pub, but I was increasingly aware that I had to make a decision about whom I should follow – God or me. The double life I was leading was no longer enough; it no longer satisfied. For the first time I began, in some small way, to understand the meaning of Jesus' death on the cross. Before, the cross had been just a religious symbol without meaning. Now I began to see it as a symbol of God's love, mercy and grace. **I felt God had pursued me all these years and that I couldn't delay in responding any longer.**

I went to my Chinese-Malaysian friend's room, and with tears rolling down my cheeks, I confessed that I had ignored God. At that moment I trusted in Jesus' death to pay the penalty of my rebellion. Suddenly, a sense of elation gripped me. I knew this Jesus to be true to His word, bringing forgiveness, goodness and mercy. A great sense of awe and love filled my heart. I ran to the phone and called my mother and sister: 'I've become a Christian!' I told them. They were bewildered, not knowing how to respond.

My friends and I started a weekly Bible study and by the end of the term we had twelve people meeting for daily prayer. What a joy – we had people from all different countries meeting together, praising God. Although I had friends from school who I had known for thirteen years, my new friends were really special. They were a great blessing, and remain so today.

My lifestyle didn't change overnight though. I still tried to continue as I had always done – in control of my own affairs, doing the things I liked to do. I remember going to a nightclub with one of my old drinking friends and talking to him of what God had done for me. I suddenly felt an overwhelming sense of grief as I looked around and saw men and women obviously drunk. I felt in a small way what God must feel as He sees His plans for deep and intimate love between man and woman turned into something awful and superficial. I remember feeling physically sick and, for the first time, feeling extremely out of place there.

Up to this point I had also been a nationalist of sorts. My upbringing had instilled in me a sense of pride and solidarity with India. Now my first allegiance was with God. I didn't see myself primarily as Indian but as a Christian, allied to my Christian brothers and sisters throughout the world. I was equally at home in Britain, India or wherever God wanted me to be.

Life changed. The Bible came out from under my pillow and I started reading it and studying it with friends. Now I knew its words were true; the only puzzle was how people could reject or deny its power. This was something that I had done myself for many years, but now I was a changed person. Despite the rituals of religion which I had involved myself in, this was something radically different. I was in a personal friendship with Almighty God, the Creator of the world and now He was my personal Saviour. He had rescued me from the punishment I deserved. Now I was forgiven, my wrong living paid for and forgotten – in God's eyes I wasn't just a religious person, but I was His.

My mother continued to have periods in hospital and my family continued to have difficulty coping with the past and with forgiveness. While I continued to struggle with this, I saw in Jesus the one who cried out to God to forgive those who tortured and executed Him. He has given me peace through the troubled times. He has and continues to bless me and I continue to rely upon Him to guide and direct me. Since becoming a Christian, God has led me through many valleys but His love strengthens me. Tomorrow may be the valley of the shadow of death but like David I can say of God, 'I will fear no evil, for you are with me.'[32]

Since graduating Matt has moved back to England, and is a paediatric registrar in Leeds. He is married (to Ali) with two children.

---

[32] Psalm 23:4

Jeiran, Azerbaijan

'I was lost. A battle was raging inside me'

I was lost. With no signposts or directions to follow I admitted to myself that I was in a dreadful situation. I didn't know where I was, and I certainly had no idea where I was going. Not knowing my final destination worried me more than anything. I was leaving home, becoming an adult, and yet my life seemed like it was a road heading nowhere. I wanted direction and a destination. How could I have one? How could anyone have one?

My parents were atheists who scorned anything religious, and so they had no time for the nominal Islamic beliefs that the majority of our friends in Azerbaijan held. I wasn't prepared to rule things out so quickly. **Something had to be out there – didn't it?** I certainly believed that when things weren't going well. I would often say a quick prayer in my head when I was having a bad day. It was worth a try. If something or someone was out there then maybe they would hear my prayer and help me out.

I hoped that there was a powerful, eternal being who I could one day know personally, who would fill the dreadful void that raged through my life like a tornado.

Whether or not I would ever find it remained to be seen, but I was certainly willing to look into the possibility.

* * *

Arriving in Newcastle on a crisp autumn afternoon was the beginning of something significant in my life. Whilst I had the opportunity to experience aspects of English culture and develop my vocabulary, more importantly, I had the chance to explore if there was something more out there. I think it was the first time in my life that I had the opportunity to look over the arguments of those who believed in Jesus. I soon became a regular at the Globe Café, which took place every week and enjoyed meeting with other internationals. Most big universities in the UK have a café like this, which is run by the students involved in the Christian Union.

As I talked to the Christian students, week after week, I brought the conversation back to my fear of death. I guess I was like most people – death frightened me. Even as a girl I had been terrified. It wasn't just my possible cause of death that made me anxious, but what might happen afterwards too; this made me break out into cold sweats. I knew Christians believed in a place called heaven, and judging on what I had been told about it, it sounded a lovely place to go at the end of life. But I wasn't sure – I wasn't even sure if their God existed, let alone this perfect place called heaven. A battle was raging inside me. One day I was keen to make sure I was going to heaven; and yet the next, I fiercely denied that God ever existed. People must have thought that I was so silly, changing from one viewpoint to another!

I began going along to church to find out more about what the Bible said. As I spent more time with friends at church and the Globe Café I realised just how lovely

Christian people can be. They were so friendly, helpful and generous. Bearing in mind I had come all the way from Azerbaijan, they made me feel like I was one of them, welcoming me into their homes and lives. And yet I knew that being nice didn't make their religious beliefs right. That wasn't enough. And anyway, **as far as I saw it, I was a nice person.** I hadn't killed anyone, so therefore I hadn't done anything wrong. **I couldn't escape the fact though, that these people were different. They weren't like me, or rather, I wasn't like them.**

* * *

As I began to explore Christianity, the evidence was beginning to build. I had always been quite open to listen to different faiths and opinions, to see whether what they said was true. Despite my parents' scepticism, I didn't want to rule religion out without investigating it fully.

It was then that I saw it, the little red booklet with the words 'Why Jesus?' on the front. It was asking my question. Intrigued, I picked up a copy as I left the Globe Café that afternoon. I thought it looked interesting and I hoped it might answer some of the remaining questions that I had.

I read it that evening. I was suddenly convinced that the story of Jesus was what I had been searching for all along. I had longed that I might know the creator of this world personally; this leaflet said I could. It talked of how 'even the closest human relationships, wonderful though they are, do not in themselves satisfy this "emptiness deep inside."'[33] It's only through a life-filled relationship with the Creator God that we can know a satisfying,

---

[33] Nicky Gumbel, *Why Jesus?* (London: Alpha International, 2005), p. 3

fulfilling relationship; for this is why we were made. It went on to explain that the Bible teaches that the reason we feel so empty, unable to rest, is because we have turned our backs on God. In doing so, we have walked away from the only One that can satisfy our deepest hunger and thirst – not a physical hunger and thirst, but one which involves our desire for meaning, purpose, life, but ultimately forgiveness.[34] I read on wanting to know more.

Classing myself as a sinner wasn't something I was prepared to do before, but as I read about how the Bible views mankind, I knew that I was a sinful person. God cannot accept anything less than perfection because He is perfect. That night, I realised I was as far away from perfect as I could be. I had no hope if God only accepted perfect people. There were many little things I'd done wrong – but even these were too much for a pure, holy God. It terrified me. The concept of a sinless God seeing me in my dreadful state scared me. If He punished me forever I couldn't complain.

No wonder I was empty inside. The God who created me was a million miles away, because I had cut Him out of my life by doing what I wanted, rather than what He wanted. As I looked back at the emptiness in my life I knew I had brought nothing but trouble upon myself. And it was entirely my fault.

I wanted to do something about it. Turn back time; change my mind; undo the wrong in my life – anything, but I couldn't. None of us can. Thankfully, God loves us so much that He did something about it for us. I learned how God came to earth in the form of a human. A perfect man – Jesus. He never did anything wrong. He was different from anyone before Him and anyone after Him.

---

[34] See John chapters 4 and 6

But what He did when He died was amazing, radical and potentially life-changing for every human – He provided a way back to having a relationship with God.

What I read was mind-blowing. Jesus obeyed the desire of His Father and took the punishment for sin that we deserve on Himself. While being executed by Roman soldiers He was isolated from His Father for the first time. In so doing Jesus was taking the judgment sentence that we deserve for turning our backs on God and His commands.

As I turned over the final page of the booklet I realised that I could be accepted back by God. It was what I longed for, and it was all made possible by Jesus' willingness to die in my place – taking the punishment that should have been mine. If I would only admit my sin to God, trust Him that His death was enough to remove the punishment I deserved, and dedicate my life to living His way rather than mine, then new life could be mine.

That is exactly what I did. As I sat in my room, I closed the booklet and put it down on my bed. 'God, I don't know that much about you, but I know you died for me and want to save me. Please will you do that? I'm embarrassed about how I have lived – about how wrong my attitude towards you has been. Please forgive me, and now help me to follow you, and live your way not mine. Thank you.'

It was the best decision of my life. I am filled with joy that I cannot explain. Even though life can still be tough, nothing compares to knowing God personally. **My void is filled and I have purpose in my life that I never imagined I could have.**

Jeiran is currently working in Newcastle. However, after a recent trip back to the Middle East she has not ruled out the possibility of returning to her home country.

Leanne, Finland

'My mind was numb. I was always either drunk or hung-over'

Leanne sat back on her bed, resting her head against the wall. Her body was tired, her mind vacant, and her forehead tense with anxiety. She drew another drag from the spliff, inhaling deeply before slowly exhaling, waiting for the calming effects of the drug. How had she got like this? And more importantly, what could she do about it now?

* * *

Leanne was born in the city of Espoo in southern Finland. Like most families in Finland her parents held strong religious beliefs and attended a Lutheran Church. And so, as was the custom, Leanne was baptised as a baby.

To most people, Leanne was an unassuming girl who was a pleasure to be around. However, she was not without ambition and determination. It was during her teenage years that things began to change. No doubt the long, dark months of a Scandinavian winter played their part, but Leanne started to become less fun to hang around with. It began when she was fourteen with bullying one of her friends. It took everyone by surprise – Leanne included. Just what was driving her to this kind of behaviour?

It wasn't long before the oppressive winter period was affecting her mind too. Already she had become despondent. She could see no way out. Like many teenagers she felt trapped in her own body. This frustration and dissatisfaction was evident on Leanne's face. Her gentle smile had now been replaced with a hardened frown.

At the age of fifteen, it was time for Leanne to be confirmed, a re-dedication of her baptism as a baby.

*'It didn't make sense because my confirmation appeared to be more to do with my age than my religious belief. **Looking back, it was simply a stage in my life: being confirmed seemed to be the right thing to do. For me, it was empty and meaningless.'***

Leanne felt ashamed that she couldn't be more honest, especially since the ceremony would be conducted in a church – supposedly under the watchful eye of Almighty God. But nobody had ever asked her about her relationship with God; until they did, Leanne was not going to cause concern or controversy by stating her irreligious state of mind.

* * *

Later that month Leanne began secondary school. Despite its location, Ressu Upper Secondary School rejected anything below excellent. It was keen to keep its reputation as one of the best in Finland. It was here that things became more competitive. Leanne was used to doing extremely well in all her classes and so was disappointed when she realised that her peers were surpassing even *her* results. This led to Leanne showing a disinterest in her work. She never let the standard drop significantly, but allowed herself enough time away from work to fall in love with a good-looking guy.

Unfortunately, he was somebody who was interested only in what he could gain. For him it was all about having sex. Leanne obliged. Sex was nothing; she would have done anything for him, for she was totally in love. But the torture of an ungrateful, unloving boyfriend eventually became too much. He remained dissatisfied. She was sick and tired of being taken for granted. She left him, and left herself heartbroken.

The pain ripped through her as though she was being stabbed. Leanne was desperate for a means of escape, which she found through immersing herself thoroughly in her work. Second year of college came and went, but not without a serious amount of study being done. The results matched the effort, even though hobbies such as horse riding had to be left behind.

Leanne explains the attitude she had towards her work: *'I was looking for acceptance through it. I wanted to be liked, hoping that getting top grades would aid this. I felt I couldn't get recognition any other way. Foolishly, I opted to extend my studies into four years instead of the usual three. So when it came to my fourth year in college both my friends and hobbies had gone and I was left with nothing to do but study. I felt awful.'*

Despite her feelings however, Leanne was still a major achiever – one of the best in her class. As a result, she was selected to represent Finland at the International Biology Olympiad in Belarus later that summer. Not satisfied, she also won a national German essay writing competition. Later, she received a language award in Austria too. Academically, Leanne had made it, and yet looking back she describes that time as being *'one of the emptiest and loneliest times of my life.'* As a form of escape, she would often borrow one of her older friend's ID cards which enabled her to go clubbing with some older friends she had made. Getting drunk soon won Leanne acceptance by the group. Unfortunately, it wasn't long before the fake ID was spotted; she was caught. And so the clubbing and drinking were brought to an abrupt end. Thrown out of clubs and left out in the cold forced Leanne to accept the lonely state from which she had tried to escape.

'I felt ugly and horrible,' she remembers. *'I would wake up in the morning desperate to hide under my duvet all day. I wished no-one would have to look at me. I hoped that one day the walls of my bedroom would collapse, falling in around me, bringing my miserable life to an end. I resented leaving the house.'*

Leanne was now regularly self-harming – hitting and scratching her body until blood dripped from her veins and onto her bed sheets. She was desperate for a release. Perhaps she could disappear one day, leaving no trace of where she had gone. That way she could start again. That would help for a while, wouldn't it?

Her whole life was falling apart. She wasn't overweight, yet she felt so fat that she stopped eating – until her weight dropped alarmingly. Her world was in turmoil. However, in all of this she never let the one thing she was proud of slip: her college grades.

* * *

For some time, Leanne had been thinking of going away to university. Germany was her first and only choice; England had certainly not crossed her mind. Not until that is, she met someone special.

Her father, who had separated from her mother when she was still at secondary school, had booked a short holiday for the two of them to catch up on. Unfortunately, just before they were meant to leave Leanne received a call; her father was unable to go. Disappointed, she quickly made some phone calls of her own, and before long, a good friend from college stepped in and took her father's place.

The two of them set off for the Canary Islands for what promised to be a wild time: clubs, alcohol and guys. For the first time in a while Leanne felt alive again. She soaked up the sun, drank cocktails and enjoyed the view (of men!). It was as though she had left all her worries behind. It was then that the inevitable happened. Leanne met someone.

* * *

Matthew was from England, and he quickly persuaded Leanne to move there with him. He seemed a nice bloke, generous with his money: he even paid for Leanne's flight over to England. Leanne felt herself falling in love. Once in England, they moved in together, and Leanne felt free from her burdens once more. Well, at least she thought she was free. The reality was she was just too busy to let them depress her again.

It was some months later, after Matthew had been over to stay in Finland, that his true colours began to show. *'It turned out that not everything was as he had first said. His housemate was in trouble with the police, which left us in a tricky situation. Matthew failed to give me assurances for the future – the assurance I badly needed. I was fed up with living life on the edge of uncertainty. It was like it was when I was back in college, feeling fat, alone and at times afraid. All the same, he was extremely possessive, and was afraid that I would leave him. I wanted to give him time, but I couldn't give him forever... It was later that summer that I decided I had had enough, and so I packed up my bags and left Matthew for good.'*

* * *

Two months after leaving Matthew, Leanne did something she had never thought she would – she began her studies at an English university. At nineteen years of age, she took her place at the University of Warwick to study Microbiology and Virology.

'It was great to have so many new people around me. I loved it. I'd go out every night. I felt free and attractive with no worries. My drunkenness left my mind numb. I was always either drunk or hung-over. I missed at least a third of the lectures, but the first year was so easy that I still got a first. Like most university students, I had a few flings with different guys and even had one with a girl. I suppose I was still looking for acceptance, but I still hadn't found it, which annoyed me. There was a Christian girl, Jenny, on my course and we started talking about Christianity when we were out one night. I was drunk as ever, which was probably why we got talking about Christianity! That night, to my surprise she prayed for me, and gave me her Bible. **I walked back to my halls drunk, holding the Bible in one hand and a bottle of vodka in the other! I must have looked a state!**

'The next morning I woke up late. As I was extremely hung over I missed my nine o'clock lecture. There was only one thing to do – start drinking again, which I did: I opened up another bottle of vodka. It wasn't even eleven o'clock. Drinking wasn't unusual for me, but reading the Bible as I drank was. Despite my drunken state, what I was reading made some sense. I was, however, worried about the things I would have to give up if I followed Jesus, and so I tried to put it out of my mind.

'However, Jenny kept inviting me to Christian Union meetings and church. Although my initial reaction was to decline, I did accept her invites, and went along. To my surprise, I met lots of happy, sociable people there, some of *whom I already knew from my hall. Prior to that I thought Christians were all serious, boring people. I also finally began to realise how important Jesus is to Christians. God is not a nice big fluffy thing in the sky, but God, someone who wants to have a living relationship with me. It was all making sense; yet I was scared and reluctant to believe.*

'I did have one problem with Christians though – I found the attitude of the Bible towards pre-marital sex and homosexual relationships really off-putting. I couldn't understand why God would be so restrictive. Why put a dampener on things? To me it seemed as though He was out to spoil our fun, and I didn't like the judgmental aspect of the Bible's view of relationships outside marriage. This was particularly hard to accept because of my recent relationship with Matthew. I thought that the Bible in this respect was particularly outdated and irrelevant.

'It all seemed good and interesting to a point, but I knew that if I was ever to become a Christian, and live life God's way, there would have to be a dramatic change in my life. I just wasn't prepared for that. Not yet.

'The summer after my first year at Warwick I did an internship in Berlin at the Robert-Koch Institute. One afternoon a group of Christians came to my halls of residence to talk about Jesus. Quite bizarrely, it turned out that one of them, Sally, was to go to Warwick University later that year. We decided to stay in touch.

'Over the following months we spent hours talking about faith and God, but I kept convincing myself that I'd never become a Christian because I didn't want such a big commitment in my life. But then I wasn't exactly happy as I was. Perhaps it was worth investigating a little further.

*'***My mind was too tired to consider such a serious decision. I was worn out with all the partying. Somehow drinking no longer gave me the fulfilment it once did.*** It seemed dull. Although I had been very anti-drugs all my life, cannabis*

became a serious temptation as it was easily available. I was curious. I was also bored with drinking, so I decided to give it a go. It was much nicer than alcohol and gave me the feeling of fulfilment I had been longing for.

'After a while, cannabis failed to give me the buzz it once had. What was I to do? – neither drugs nor alcohol did it for me anymore. I was more disillusioned than ever before. I hadn't stopped reading the Bible though: to my surprise I came to the conclusion that nothing was going to satisfy me but Jesus. So many coincidences, such as meeting the Christians in my hall and meeting Jenny convinced me that God was directing my life. My lecturers were telling me how amazing all the biological mechanisms were, and I began thinking to myself that whoever created them would have to be very powerful, if not a genius.

'As I read more of the Bible it provided me with more and more evidence that Jesus really is the Son of God. But even with all the evidence and signs, the last step of faith was a massive leap. I knew that I had cut God out of my life. I had gone my own way and it had left me in a mess. I was terrified, and yet I felt God was calling for me even though I was trying to hide from Him. I was so messed up and so disgusting in God's sight. The Bible tells me that He is pure. How could He ever forgive me for all my wrong doing? I felt I was not good enough for Jesus.

'I had been meeting Sally regularly for a while, and often talked about the question of giving control of my life over to God, about how hard it was to accept that He is bigger and more powerful than me. I realised that even if I convinced myself that I was in control, He would still be bigger, and would still have supreme control.

'I told Sally that I wanted to become a Christian, but that I was scared. She prayed that I might have courage and feel accepted by God. It was then, for the first time, that I really believed what was written about Jesus and the truth of it all. I

prayed a little prayer, thanking Jesus for dying for my sins. I asked Him to forgive me, and invited Him into my life. It was like a heavy load had been lifted off me! I felt so happy and excited! I had done so much wrong but I could still be forgiven for it all.

'**When I became a Christian it changed everything. For the first time in my life, I felt safe, accepted and forgiven.** *God promises He will always be there for us; that He never abandons us or lets us down and I can say that that has proved true for me.*[35] *My only regret was that I did not trust Him earlier... You gain so much compared to what you give up. In God I found the completion and acceptance I had been looking for in partying, drinking, smoking and relationships. I can now see why God gives guidelines on how we should live, and understand that these are for our own good.* **I see so many students on my campus crying out for God's love but not accepting Him. I just wish they would** *– it was the best decision I made.'*

Leanne is finishing her studies at the University of Warwick, where she is actively involved in the Christian Union.

If Leanne's story has raised some difficult issues for you and you would find it helpful to talk with someone confidentially regarding these, please contact Friends International:

Tel: +44 (0)20 8780 3511
Email: info@new2uk.org

---

[35] Hebrews 13:5; Deuteronomy 31:6

A World of Difference

Whether you have read through the whole of this book, or picked out a chapter or two that are of particular interest to you, you won't have been able to escape the fact that each story tells of how one Man has turned lives around. He has made a world of difference. And that person is... Jesus.

The question everyone needs to answer is why is Jesus so significant? Why does He transform lives so radically? The Bible tells us that He does so because He is God. Jesus was a real person in history. He lived on this earth just like you and me. But He was born like no other person – through a woman who was still a virgin. He was born because God intervened in a girl's life, created a special baby, and brought Him into the world for our sakes. Jesus is unique because He is God, coming into our world as a man.

He is not one of many gods, He is God Himself: the only God. The Bible teaches that He is above everyone and everything else.

But the question remains: how does an eternal, almighty God bring the radical change in people's lives to which this book testifies? There is a well-known verse in the Bible, which is found in John's record of Jesus' life on earth. This one verse explains to us the heart of the Christian message. This is what it says:

> For God so loved the world that he gave his only Son, that whoever believes in him shall not perish but have eternal life.[36]

In this short, simple statement is a summary of the great news of the life-changing Jesus.

Watching the television news, we often see natural disasters and man-made tragedies unfold. In our own personal experience too, we experience grief and hurt. At such times, it can be easy to conclude that God does not care about or love us. We can begin to feel that God is distant, detached and unfriendly, with no concern for the world today. Perhaps, we wonder, God only loves those who are special or perfect. This verse from the Bible, spoken by Jesus Himself, confirms that this is not the case. Rather, Jesus expresses God's perfect, complete and eternal love for the world, which He had created.

Examining the verse, we see three vitally important truths.

First, when God loves, He loves the world.

The Bible leaves no room for us to doubt whether God loves us. He loves us, not because we are good, or because we have lived our lives in the way He wants us to, but because we are made by Him, and He loves us despite all our wrong doing. The Bible says that, 'God demonstrates his own love for us in this: While we were still sinners, Christ died for us.'[37] For God to send Jesus to earth to die for us is His greatest demonstration of God's love. It was when we were at our worst, when we were far away from God, that He proved His own love for us

---

[36] John 3:16
[37] Romans 5:8

by coming to our rescue. We didn't deserve it, yet He gave Himself for us, because He loves us.

All humanity the world over does that which is wrong. We break God's commandments. We don't love God as we should. Neither do we love others as we ought. The Bible calls this sin, and it is this that cuts us off from God who is perfect and without sin. But still, God came to this world for us. The Bible says that, 'Jesus came into the world to save sinners.'[38] That couldn't include any more people, for it includes everyone. Jesus died for the sin of all people of all time – from every civilisation, culture and country. Whatever our national or religious background we have all rejected God and His design for this world. The Bible teaches that the whole world is lost. It is as if we are wandering around, hoping that with some luck we might find the right way to go. Jesus came to look for and save those who are lost, because He loves us.

Secondly, when God gives, He gives His Son.

When a person *really* loves someone it is fair to imagine that they would give them the things that are most precious. For example, suppose you love somebody, wouldn't you buy them special presents for their birthday? A man who loves a woman would buy her an expensive ring or necklace to demonstrate how he has been captivated by her love. However, the most precious thing that anyone can give as an expression of their love is their own life. There is nothing more that people can give. That is exactly what God did for us. He gave to us what was most precious to Him – His life.

Jonathan from France and Nicola from Saudi Arabia, like many others, came to a realisation that every person has done wrong in the sight of God. The Bible describes

---

[38] 1 Timothy 1:15

it as 'fall[ing] short of the glory of God.'[39] We do not meet God's standard. None of us compares to God, for He is perfect. This leaves us with a major problem, because though God is a God of love, He is equally just. He cannot simply ignore our sin, for that would be unfair. As we want justice to take place when someone does wrong against us, so God insists that those who do wrong must be punished. Sinful people are not only mass-murderers and serial rapists. In God's eyes we are all guilty of breaking God's standard for the world He has made. Let me explain.

Imagine you had bought a lovely new white shirt or top. It was spotlessly clean and looked amazing because of its pure white colour. If however, you drew a mark on your sleeve with a permanent pen the whole shirt would be ruined, even if the mark was very small. The wrong things we do are like the mark on that shirt – however small we may believe them to be, they spoil things between us and the God who is pure and holy. Therefore sin cannot be ignored.

If God overlooked these things He wouldn't be fair, and couldn't be a loving God. God takes sin so seriously that if we fail to acknowledge our wrong to Him, and continue to live for ourselves, we will have to face God's justice. The Bible makes it clear that punishment is something that we deserve.

This is where God proves His love for us. Out of total goodness and love, God came to our rescue through Jesus coming to earth. God took on Himself the figure of a perfect human being.

Jesus came to die as a substitute for us. However hard we may try to remove the dirty marks of sin from our lives, we cannot do it. No amount of good things or

---

[39] Romans 3:23

religious activity will change the past. The only possible way is to receive forgiveness. This is exactly what God offers to us as a gift. Jesus, the Son of God came to earth to die and take on Himself our sin. He paid the penalty that it would take us all eternity to pay; He carried our sin on Himself as He hung and died on the cross.

Thirdly, when God saves He saves forever.

Jesus came to this earth for one distinct and definite purpose: He came to save. He came to save you and me from the separation of God that our wrong has brought upon us. The only possible way He could do this was to swap places with us: for Him, a man who never did *anything* wrong, to be punished for all our wrong.

Imagine that you had committed a dreadful crime, and there was no escape. Everyone knew that you were guilty. The penalty for your crime was death. As you faced the judge ready to be sentenced, you knew the end had come. However, as the judge was reading out your sentence someone in the court room spoke up and said that they would take your place. They would be put to death, and you would be allowed to go free! Just imagine it; it would seem too good to be true. But that is what Jesus did for us, only in a greater way. Two thousand years ago, He allowed Himself to be put to death on a cross. He was taking our punishment. He died, was buried, and then, three days later, He did what no other human has ever done. He rose from the dead and proved this by appearing to literally hundreds of people. He had accomplished what we could never achieve for ourselves. He died to set us free, to forgive us, to give us the opportunity to be reunited with the God we were created to know and enjoy. He was saving us from what we deserve. What we need to do is receive the free gift that He offers.

That is exactly what every person in this book has done: Leanne, Jeiran, Yu-re and the others. It hasn't made a difference what part of the world they are from: they have all accepted that they have done wrong in the eyes of God. They have realised that because God is fair and just, they deserved punishment. However, Jesus stood in their place and gave them the opportunity to go free. They have all accepted His perfect and lasting offer. They have come to know God, and have everlasting life. They know God now, and will be with Him throughout life, through death, and into eternity. God, as their Heavenly Father, will keep them close to Him. They are saved… forever!

As several in the book have pointed out, He doesn't just bridge the gap between us and God, and then leave us to go it alone. Because God loves us so much, He wants to remain with us, help us, and change us. When Jesus left earth to return to heaven, He promised two things: first, that in the same way He left this earth, He would also come back and return to it;[40] second, He promised that He would be with us – always until the end of the age.[41] He remains with us by giving us the Holy Spirit. The Holy Spirit is an equal member of the Godhead, who brings about the change noticeable in the life of a Christian. The Spirit points us to God, enabling us to live for Him.

We cannot change ourselves, but it is only through the power of God that we can be changed. This answers the question of how God can bring about a change in the lives of you and me. First, He provides a way back to God through the death of Jesus. Jesus acts as our mediator, to enable us to be reunited into a perfect relationship with

---

[40] John 14:3
[41] Matthew 28:20

God. God then gives us His Spirit to help us, lead and change us. The Bible describes it as being 'conformed into His likeness'[42] – not that we ever become equal to God, or can work our way to God, but we want to become like Him.

As we have seen, following Jesus can be extremely hard, but God promises to help us and give us the strength to do what is right.[43]

* * *

In this book the true stories of people from around the world have been uncovered. The real-life account of how Jesus has changed their lives has been told. You will not have been able to escape the obvious transformation that Jesus makes to someone's life. But what will you do? Will you accept Jesus as your Lord and Saviour, or will you carry on without God throughout life, and for eternity? Will you allow Jesus to become the commander of your life?

It doesn't matter where in the world you are from, where you have been or what you have done: Jesus came to rescue you because He loves you. Will you, today, accept His offer of free, everlasting forgiveness?

Many have found that praying a prayer like the one below has helped them put their trust in Jesus, and accept God's gift of forgiveness:

> God in heaven, I admit that I have done things wrong which need Your forgiveness. I want to turn away from all my sin. Please forgive me. I believe that Jesus took the punishment I deserve, and has

---

[42] Romans 8:29
[43] Luke 9:23

allowed me to go free. I invite You to become Lord and Saviour of my life. Please change me so that I become more like You. By Your Holy Spirit come and live in my life. Help me to follow You. Thank You for loving me and hearing this prayer. I pray in the name of Jesus, Amen.

If you would like help in starting to live as a Christian or simply want to discuss the issues raised in this book, please email info@new2uk.org.

By contacting Friends International on the email address above, they will also be able to give you information about courses that are being run in your area that will help you investigate the person of Jesus in more depth. It is an excellent way of uncovering the truth for yourself, and I would encourage you to do so if you are serious about wanting to have a real friendship and unity with God.

Further Reading

Answers to Tough Questions, Josh McDowell and Don Stewart (Milton Keynes: Authentic Media, 2006)

Challenging Catholics, John Martin and Dwight Longenecker (Carlisle: Paternoster Press, 2001)

Christianity Explored, Rico Tice and Barry Cooper (Surrey: The Good Book Company, 2005)

Fresh Start, J.C. Chapman (London: Hodder and Stoughton, 1986)

Real Lives, D.J. Carswell (Milton Keynes: Authentic Media, 2004, reprinted)

Turning Points, Vaughan Roberts (Milton Keynes: Authentic Media, 2006, reprinted)

Uncovered, Jonathan Carswell (Milton Keynes: Authentic Media, 2006, reprinted)

Why Believe? Roger Carswell (Milton Keynes: Authentic Media, 2004, reprinted)

Why Should God Bother with Me? Simon Austen (Tain: Christian Focus, 2002)

About Friends International

An estimated one million international students come to the UK each year. Many receive a warm welcome from their universities. However, they still face a unique collection of issues: language difficulties, culture shock, homesickness and often loneliness.

A recent UK survey of international students discovered that only 15 percent of Chinese students had British friends. Almost 60 percent of those surveyed indicated a positive desire to experience UK culture and family life. The majority claimed that making friends with UK students and others from the local community was one of the most positive aspects of their time in the country.

Friends International is a Christian organisation which understands that being an international student can be an exciting and useful time, but that it can also be frustrating and lonely.

With over 60 staff workers in 30 different cities the organisation serves international students by offering them unconditional friendship, genuine hospitality and the opportunity to learn about Jesus Christ. Friends International welcomes students of any faith – and those without, and can be contacted using any of the details below.

Friends International
3 Crescent Stables
139 Upper Richmond Road
London
SW15 2TN

Tel: 020 8780 3511
Email: info@new2uk.org
Web: www.friendsinternational.org.uk

friends
INTERNATIONAL

- 🌏 New 2 the UK?
- 🌏 Want to meet British people?
- 🌏 Want to find out about British culture and customs?
- 🌏 Want to practise your English?
- 🌏 Contact us!

To find out what's going on near you...
Tel: +44 (0)20 8780 3511
Email: info@new2uk.org
...or visit our website at
www.new2uk.org

New 2 UK?

You've probably been attracted to the UK by the vibrant culture and the opportunity to gain a qualification that will be respected worldwide. Many UK universities and colleges provide a warm welcome for international students. However it's still not easy adjusting to a new life away from home. you'll face a whole host of issues: a different language, exciting new experiences, culture shock, and perhaps even homesickness.

Friends International is a Christian organisation that helps international students of all faiths or none throughout the UK. Our services, offered unconditionally, include:

Welcome events
Hospitality schemes
English conversation practice
Opportunities to investigate the Christian faith
International cafés
Social programmes

Key Passages in the Bible

(All taken from NLT)

Christians believe that the Bible is one of the ways that God communicates directly to humans. By reading the Bible we can learn more about Him and His character. The Bible also reveals great amounts about us too. Anyone who reads the Bible with an open mind, asking God, the Holy Spirit to help them understand what God is saying will discover that God is a God who loves to talk with the people He has created. The Bible says He longs to be 'in communion' with us – that is to have a friendship and relationship.

If you have never read the Bible before and are puzzled as to where to start, here are some key Bible passages that might help you as you begin to read what God has had written down for us to read.

Genesis 1

The Account of Creation

In the beginning God created the heavens and the earth. The earth was empty, a formless mass cloaked in darkness. And the Spirit of God was hovering over its surface. Then God said, "Let there be light," and there was light. And God saw that it was good. Then he separated the light from the darkness. God called the light "day" and the darkness "night." Together these made up one day.

And God said, "Let there be space between the waters, to separate water from water." And so it was. God made this space to separate the waters above from the waters below. And God called the space "sky." This happened on the second day.

And God said, "Let the waters beneath the sky be gathered into one place so dry ground may appear." And so it was. God named the dry ground "land" and the water "seas." And God saw that it was good. Then God said, "Let the land burst forth with every sort of grass and seed-bearing plant. And let there be trees that grow seed-bearing fruit. The seeds will then produce the kinds of plants and trees from which they came." And so it was. The land was filled with seed-bearing plants and trees, and their seeds produced plants and trees of like kind. And God saw that it was good. This all happened on the third day.

And God said, "Let bright lights appear in the sky to separate the day from the night. They will be signs to mark off the seasons, the days, and the years. Let their light shine down upon the earth." And so it was. For God made two great lights, the sun and the moon, to shine down upon the earth. The greater one, the sun, presides during the day; the lesser one, the moon, presides through the night. He also made the stars. God set these lights in the heavens to light the earth, to govern the day and the night, and to separate the light from the darkness. And God saw that it was good. This all happened on the fourth day.

And God said, "Let the waters swarm with fish and other life. Let the skies be filled with birds of every kind." So God created great sea creatures and every sort of fish and every kind of bird. And God saw that it was good. Then God blessed them, saying, "Let the fish multiply and fill the oceans. Let the birds increase and fill the earth." This all happened on the fifth day.

And God said, "Let the earth bring forth every kind of animal—livestock, small animals, and wildlife." And so it was. God made all sorts of wild animals, livestock, and small animals, each able to reproduce more of its own kind. And God saw that it was good.

Then God said, "Let us make people in our image, to be like ourselves. They will be masters over all life—the fish in the sea, the birds in the sky, and all the livestock, wild animals, and small animals."

So God created people in his own image; God patterned them after himself; male and female he created them. God blessed them and told them, "Multiply and fill the earth and subdue it. Be masters over the fish and birds and all the animals." And God said, "Look! I have given you the seed-bearing plants throughout the earth and all the fruit trees for your food. And I have given all the grasses and other green plants to the animals and birds for their food." And so it was. Then God looked over all he had made, and he saw that it was excellent in every way. This all happened on the sixth day.

Genesis 3

The Man and Woman Sin

Now the serpent was the shrewdest of all the creatures the LORD God had made. "Really?" he asked the woman. "Did God really say you must not eat any of the fruit in the garden?"

"Of course we may eat it," the woman told him. "It's only the fruit from the tree at the centre of the garden that we are not allowed to eat. God says we must not eat it or even touch it, or we will die."

"You won't die!" the serpent hissed. "God knows that your eyes will be opened when you eat it. You will become just like God, knowing everything, both good and evil."

The woman was convinced. The fruit looked so fresh and delicious, and it would make her so wise! So she ate some of the fruit. She also gave some to her husband, who was with her. Then he ate it, too. At that moment, their eyes were opened, and they suddenly felt shame at their nakedness. So they strung fig leaves together around their hips to cover themselves.

Toward evening they heard the LORD God walking about in the garden, so they hid themselves among the trees. The LORD God called to Adam, "Where are you?"

He replied, "I heard you, so I hid. I was afraid because I was naked."

"Who told you that you were naked?" the LORD God asked. "Have you eaten the fruit I commanded you not to eat?"

"Yes," Adam admitted, "but it was the woman you gave me who brought me the fruit, and I ate it."

Then the LORD God asked the woman, "How could you do such a thing?"

"The serpent tricked me," she replied. "That's why I ate it."...Then God said to the woman, "You will bear children with intense pain and suffering. And though your desire will be for your husband, he will be your master."

And to Adam he said, "Because you listened to your wife and ate the fruit I told you not to eat, I have placed a curse on the ground. All your life you will struggle to scratch a living from it. It will grow thorns and thistles for you, though you will eat of its grains. All your life you will sweat to produce food, until your dying day. Then you will return to the ground from which you came. For you were made from dust, and to the dust you will return."

Then Adam named his wife Eve, because she would be the mother of all people everywhere. And the LORD God made clothing from animal skins for Adam and his wife.

Then the LORD God said, "The people have become as we are, knowing everything, both good and evil. What if they eat the fruit of the tree of life? Then they will live forever!" So the LORD God banished Adam and his wife from the Garden of Eden, and he sent Adam out to cultivate the ground from which he had been made. After banishing them from the garden, the LORD God stationed mighty angelic beings to the east of Eden. And a flaming sword flashed back and forth, guarding the way to the tree of life.

Psalm 23

A psalm of David

The LORD is my shepherd;
    I have everything I need.
He lets me rest in green meadows;
    he leads me beside peaceful streams.
    He renews my strength.
He guides me along right paths,
    bringing honour to his name.

Even when I walk
    through the dark valley of death,
I will not be afraid,
    for you are close beside me.
Your rod and your staff
    protect and comfort me.

You prepare a feast for me
    in the presence of my enemies.
You welcome me as a guest,
    anointing my head with oil.
    My cup overflows with blessings.
Surely your goodness and unfailing love
    will pursue me all the days of my life,

and I will live in the house of the LORD
forever.

Psalm 91

Those who live in the shelter of the Most High
will find rest in the shadow of the Almighty.
This I declare of the LORD:
    He alone is my refuge, my place of safety;
he is my God, and I am trusting him.
For he will rescue you from every trap
    and protect you from the fatal plague.
He will shield you with his wings.
    He will shelter you with his feathers.
    His faithful promises are your armour and protection.
Do not be afraid of the terrors of the night,
    nor fear the dangers of the day,
nor dread the plague that stalks in darkness,
    nor the disaster that strikes at midday.
Though a thousand fall at your side,
    though ten thousand are dying around you,
    these evils will not touch you.
But you will see it with your eyes;
    you will see how the wicked are punished.

If you make the LORD your refuge,
    if you make the Most High your shelter,
no evil will conquer you;
    no plague will come near your dwelling.
For he orders his angels
    to protect you wherever you go.
They will hold you with their hands
    to keep you from striking your foot on a stone.

You will trample down lions and poisonous snakes;
    you will crush fierce lions and serpents under your feet!

The LORD says, "I will rescue those who love me.
   I will protect those who trust in my name.
When they call on me, I will answer;
   I will be with them in trouble.
   I will rescue them and honour them.
I will satisfy them with a long life
   and give them my salvation."

Isaiah 9

Hope in the Messiah – Isaiah predicting the coming of Jesus around 700 years before His birth

For a child is born to us, a son is given to us. And the government will rest on his shoulders. These will be his royal titles: Wonderful Counsellor, Mighty God, Everlasting Father, Prince of Peace. His ever expanding, peaceful government will never end. He will rule forever with fairness and justice from the throne of his ancestor David. The passionate commitment of the LORD Almighty will guarantee this!

Isaiah 53

Who has believed our message? To whom will the LORD reveal his saving power? My servant grew up in the LORD's presence like a tender green shoot, sprouting from a root in dry and sterile ground. There was nothing beautiful or majestic about his appearance, nothing to attract us to him. He was despised and rejected—a man of sorrows, acquainted with bitterest grief. We turned our backs on him and looked the other way when he went by. He was despised, and we did not care.

Yet it was our weaknesses he carried; it was our sorrows that weighed him down. And we thought his troubles were a punishment from God for his own sins! But he was wounded and crushed for our sins. He was beaten that we might have peace. He was whipped, and we were healed! All of us have strayed away like sheep. We have left God's paths to follow our own. Yet the LORD laid on him the guilt and sins of us all.

He was oppressed and treated harshly, yet he never said a word. He was led as a lamb to the slaughter. And as a sheep is silent before the shearers, he did not open his mouth. From prison and trial they led him away to his death. But who among the people realized that he was dying for their sins—that he was suffering their punishment? He had done no wrong, and he never deceived anyone. But he was buried like a criminal; he was put in a rich man's grave.

But it was the LORD's good plan to crush him and fill him with grief. Yet when his life is made an offering for sin, he will have a multitude of children, many heirs. He will enjoy a long life, and the LORD's plan will prosper in his hands. When he sees all that is accomplished by his anguish, he will be satisfied. And because of what he has experienced, my righteous servant will make it possible for many to be counted righteous, for he will bear all their sins. I will give him the honours of one who is mighty and great, because he exposed himself to death. He was counted among those who were sinners. He bore the sins of many and interceded for sinners.

Luke 2

The Birth of Jesus
At that time the Roman emperor, Augustus, decreed that a census should be taken throughout the Roman Empire. (This was the first census taken when Quirinius was governor of Syria.) All returned to their own towns to register for this census. And because Joseph was a descendant of King David, he had to go to Bethlehem in

Judea, David's ancient home. He travelled there from the village of Nazareth in Galilee. He took with him Mary, his fiancée, who was obviously pregnant by this time.

And while they were there, the time came for her baby to be born. She gave birth to her first child, a son. She wrapped him snugly in strips of cloth and laid him in a manger, because there was no room for them in the village inn.

The Shepherds and Angels
That night some shepherds were in the fields outside the village, guarding their flocks of sheep. Suddenly, an angel of the Lord appeared among them, and the radiance of the Lord's glory surrounded them. They were terribly frightened, but the angel reassured them. "Don't be afraid!" he said. "I bring you good news of great joy for everyone! The Saviour—yes, the Messiah, the Lord—has been born tonight in Bethlehem, the city of David! And this is how you will recognize him: You will find a baby lying in a manger, wrapped snugly in strips of cloth!"

Suddenly, the angel was joined by a vast host of others—the armies of heaven—praising God: "Glory to God in the highest heaven, and peace on earth to all whom God favours." When the angels had returned to heaven, the shepherds said to each other, "Come on, let's go to Bethlehem! Let's see this wonderful thing that has happened, which the Lord has told us about."

They ran to the village and found Mary and Joseph. And there was the baby, lying in the manger. Then the shepherds told everyone what had happened and what the angel had said to them about this child. All who heard the shepherds' story were astonished, but Mary quietly treasured these things in her heart and thought about them often. The shepherds went back to their fields and flocks, glorifying and praising God for what the angels had told them, and because they had seen the child, just as the angel had said.

Matthew 5

The Sermon on the Mount

One day as the crowds were gathering, Jesus went up the mountainside with his disciples and sat down to teach them.

This is what he taught them:

"God blesses those who realize their need for him,
   for the Kingdom of Heaven is given to them.
God blesses those who mourn, for they will be
   comforted.
God blesses those who are gentle and lowly,
   for the whole earth will belong to them.
God blesses those who are hungry and thirsty for justice,
   for they will receive it in full.
God blesses those who are merciful,
   for they will be shown mercy.
God blesses those whose hearts are pure,
   for they will see God.
God blesses those who work for peace,
   for they will be called the children of God.
God blesses those who are persecuted because they live for God,
   for the Kingdom of Heaven is theirs.

"God blesses you when you are mocked and persecuted and lied about because you are my followers. Be happy about it! Be very glad! For a great reward awaits you in heaven. And remember, the ancient prophets were persecuted, too.

John 3 v 16 – 21

"For God so loved the world that he gave his only Son, so that everyone who believes in him will not perish but have eternal life. God did not send his Son into the world to condemn it, but to save it.

"There is no judgment awaiting those who trust him. But those who do not trust him have already been judged for not believing in the only Son of God. Their judgment is based on this fact: The light from heaven came into the world, but they loved the darkness more than the light, for their actions were evil. They hate the light because they want to sin in the darkness. They stay away from the light for fear their sins will be exposed and they will be punished. But those who do what is right come to the light gladly, so everyone can see that they are doing what God wants."

Mark 15

The Crucifixion

A certain man from Cyrene, Simon, the father of Alexander and Rufus, was passing by on his way in from the country, and they forced him to carry the cross. They brought Jesus to the place called Golgotha (which means Skull Hill). Then they offered him wine mixed with myrrh, but he did not take it. And they crucified him. Dividing up his clothes, they cast lots to see what each would get.

It was the third hour when they crucified him. The written notice of the charge against him read: "The King of the Jews". They crucified two robbers with him, one on his right and one on his left. Those who passed by hurled insults at him, shaking their heads and saying, "So! You who are going to destroy the temple and build it in three days, come down from the cross and save yourself!"

In the same way the chief priests and the teachers of the law mocked him among themselves. "He saved others," they said, "but he can't save himself! Let this Christ, this King of Israel, come down now from the cross, that we may see and believe." Those crucified with him also heaped insults on him.

The Death of Jesus
At the sixth hour darkness came over the whole land until the ninth hour. And at the ninth hour Jesus cried out in a loud voice, *"Eloi, Eloi, lama sabachthani?"*—which means, "My God, my God, why have you forsaken me?" When some of those standing near heard this, they said, "Listen, he's calling Elijah." One man ran, filled a sponge with wine vinegar, put it on a stick, and offered it to Jesus to drink. "Now leave him alone. Let's see if Elijah comes to take him down," he said.

With a loud cry, Jesus breathed his last.

The curtain of the temple was torn in two from top to bottom. And when the centurion, who stood there in front of Jesus, heard his cry and saw how he died, he said, "Surely this man was the Son of God!"

Some women were watching from a distance. Among them were Mary Magdalene, Mary the mother of James the younger and of Joseph, and Salome. In Galilee these women had followed him and cared for his needs. Many other women who had come up with him to Jerusalem were also there.

The Burial of Jesus
It was Preparation Day (that is, the day before the Sabbath). So as evening approached, Joseph of Arimathea, a prominent member of the Council, who was himself waiting for the kingdom of God, went boldly to Pilate and asked for Jesus' body. Pilate was surprised to hear that he

was already dead. Summoning the centurion, he asked him if Jesus had already died. When he learned from the centurion that it was so, he gave the body to Joseph. So Joseph bought some linen cloth, took down the body, wrapped it in the linen, and placed it in a tomb cut out of rock. Then he rolled a stone against the entrance of the tomb. Mary Magdalene and Mary the mother of Joseph saw where he was laid.

John 20

The Empty Tomb

Early on the first day of the week, while it was still dark, Mary Magdalene went to the tomb and saw that the stone had been removed from the entrance. So she came running to Simon Peter and the other disciple, the one Jesus loved, and said, "They have taken the Lord out of the tomb, and we don't know where they have put him!"

So Peter and the other disciple started for the tomb. Both were running, but the other disciple outran Peter and reached the tomb first. He bent over and looked in at the strips of linen lying there but did not go in. Then Simon Peter, who was behind him, arrived and went into the tomb. He saw the strips of linen lying there, as well as the burial cloth that had been around Jesus' head. The cloth was folded up by itself, separate from the linen. Finally the other disciple, who had reached the tomb first, also went inside. He saw and believed.

Romans 5

You see, at just the right time, when we were still powerless, Christ died for the ungodly. Very rarely will anyone die for a righteous man, though for a good man someone might possibly dare to die. But God demonstrates his own love for us in this: While we were still sinners, Christ died for us.

Since we have now been justified by his blood, how much more shall we be saved from God's wrath through him! For if, when we were God's enemies, we were reconciled to him through the death of his Son, how much more, having been reconciled, shall we be saved through his life! Not only is this so, but we also rejoice in God through our Lord Jesus Christ, through whom we have now received reconciliation.

Revelation 20

John's vision of what heaven and hell will be like

And I saw an angel coming down out of heaven, having the key to the Abyss and holding in his hand a great chain. He seized the dragon, that ancient serpent, who is the devil, or Satan, and bound him for a thousand years. He threw him into the Abyss, and locked and sealed it over him, to keep him from deceiving the nations anymore until the thousand years were ended. After that, he must be set free for a short time.

I saw thrones on which were seated those who had been given authority to judge. And I saw the souls of those who had been beheaded because of their testimony for Jesus and because of the word of God. They had not worshiped the beast or his image and had not received his mark on their foreheads or their hands. They came to life and reigned with Christ a thousand years…This is the first resurrection. Blessed and holy are those who have part in the first resurrection. The second death has no power over them, but they will be priests of God and of Christ and will reign with him for a thousand years.

Satan's Doom

When the thousand years are over, Satan will be released from his prison and will go out to deceive the nations in the four corners of the earth—Gog and Magog—to gather them for battle. In number they are like the sand on the seashore. They marched across the breadth of the earth and surrounded the camp of God's people, the city he loves. But fire came down from heaven and devoured them. And the devil, who deceived them, was thrown into the lake of burning sulphur, where the beast and the false prophet had been thrown. They will be tormented day and night for ever and ever.